Marvellously easy to say, 'I get it'

A guide for anyone who wants to change lives through healthcare communications.

By Sarah Sowerby

Published by The Book Chief Publishing House 2024
(a trademark under Lydian Group Ltd)
Suite 2A, Blackthorn House, St Paul's Square,
Birmingham, B3 1RL
www.thebookchief.com

The moral right of the author has been asserted.

Text Copyright © 2024 by **Sarah Sowerby**

All rights reserved. No part of this book may be reproduced, stored in a retrieval system, or transmitted in any form or by any means, electronic, mechanical, photocopying, recording, public performances or otherwise, without written permission of **Sarah Sowerby**, except for brief quotations embodied in critical articles or reviews. The book is for personal and commercial use by the Author **Sarah Sowerby.**

The right of **Sarah Sowerby** to be identified as the author of this work has been asserted in accordance with sections 77 and 78 of the copyright Designs and Patents Act 1988.

Book Cover Design: Deearo Marketing
Editing: Laura Billingham
Typesetting / Proofreading: Sharon Brown and Ailsa Johnson
Publishing: Sharon Brown

Contents

INTRODUCTION 7

CHAPTER 1 15
WHY does it matter?

CHAPTER 2 23
7 Zones of Mastery

CHAPTER 3 25
Mastery Zone 1: codes of practice

CHAPTER 4 33
Mastery Zone 2: evidence-based writing

CHAPTER 5 49
Mastery Zone 3: translating strategy to a content plan

CHAPTER 6 59
Mastery Zone 4: producing content audiences will want to engage with

CHAPTER 7 85
Mastery Zone 5: being a 'Creative'; the power of ideas

CHAPTER 8 97
Mastery Zone 6: explaining and presenting your work - how you show up

CHAPTER 9 111
Mastery Zone 7: developing yourself and managing yourself

CHAPTER 10 121
What next?

REFERENCES 123

BEYOND 'BIKINI MEDICINE' 125

ACKNOWLEDGEMENTS 129

WORDBIRD SERVICES 131

Introduction

Hello. I'm Sarah and I am super-excited that you are reading this book because it means you are keen to learn. As a lifelong learner and 'seeker', we already have something in common. That's important to me because I hope to inspire you to create great healthcare communications in an industry I am passionate about.

I am a proud geek. I'm fascinated by the science of medicines and disease. I have spent my whole career bringing our amazing scientific stories to life through the power of creativity. I love it, and I want you to love it too. What other career can you have where content you create has the potential to change and save lives? I have primarily written this for science graduates setting out on a career in healthcare communications in the pharmaceutical industry. But anyone who manages or trains writers, is a curious client, or shares my passion for healthcare communications, is very welcome here.

What qualifies me to write this book?

I have been working in healthcare communications agencies since 1990. My copywriter career started in a small independent agency on Valentine's Day. It was love at first write!

After 3 years learning the basics (more of that later) and a rogue year as Publications Manager for stop smoking charity, QUIT, I moved to Paling Walters, now TBWA, where I spent a happy decade as Copy Chief, or 'Chiefy', as I was known.

I had the privilege of helping create some of the world's most famous prescription and over the counter brands. I was in a wonderful team. I enjoyed being deputy to my inspirational boss, the legendary Frank Walters. No wonder I stayed so long!

Eventually, with two small children and a husband who worked ridiculously long hours, it was time for me to have more life and less work.

In 2006, I set up my own freelance writing and training consultancy. Over the next six years, I worked with over 30 agencies on more amazing health brands, as a medical writer, creative writer and everything in between. It was fascinating to me how organisations doing exactly the same jobs approached the work so very differently. Like a magpie, I collected all the shiny ideas I liked and stored them away.

In 2012, things started to change. I had time with my kids, a wonderful variety of work, intellectual challenge, and fabulous clients. But something was missing. A very deep sense that my career was stagnating. That I wasn't fulfilling my potential. And after six years of working alone, I missed working in a high performing team.

I also had another problem. I had too many clients who wanted to work with me, so I turned down A LOT of business. As a lifelong people pleaser, this was very uncomfortable for me.

In the middle of the 2012 Olympics, I decided to take an office and hire a couple of science grads to train up. This gave them a foot in the door and me the capacity to help more clients and really push myself to see what was possible. I am so, so grateful to my first two grads. They took such a leap of faith to join me on that first crazy step.

I would like to tell you that everything was rainbows and unicorns from that moment onwards. But it was tough. I was EVERYTHING: Managing Director, Strategy Director, Training Director, Creative Director, Finance Director. With the help of my husband, I was even the office cleaner at weekends!

Money was tight, but I always prioritised paying my trainees over paying myself. I sincerely hope they had no idea how challenging life was for me.

Then two really significant things happened. Until that point, we were mainly working for agencies who subcontracted to us. Getting our first big pharmaceutical client was a game changer. More quickly followed, and we soon grew into a full service agency and I didn't need to do so many jobs.

The second significant thing was getting a business coach. We worked with Louisa Pau, who had co-founded Woolley Pau, sold that agency and then retrained as a coach.

I have learned so many things the hard way. And you will too. I hope this book will help accelerate your progress, enable you to ask good questions and navigate a wonderful career. Because what you produce might genuinely change, or maybe even save, someone's life.

My creds in brief

- Worked on hundreds of prescription and consumer health brands
- Devised vast amounts of core international and local UK content
- Worked with almost all pharma companies at some point in my career
- Spent much of my freelance years creating digital content
- Trained or mentored many copywriters who are now in senior agency positions or have flourishing freelance consultancies
- Founded Wordbird my own brand and creative content agency
- Created The Wordbird Copy Academy in 2012 - our much imitated training programme
- Co-Founder of Women in Pharma
- I have also been Chair of The Institute of Practitioners in Advertising (IPA) Healthcare Group, podcast cohost and I have won over 50 awards
- Self-confessed geek, 'seeker' and growth mindset enthusiast!
- I have no sense of Imposter Syndrome in writing this book

The terms I use

In this book I use the term 'healthcare copywriter' in a broad spectrum way, to cover lots of different jobs. There are lots of different types of copywriter. I have always viewed it as a spectrum stretching from medical writer to creative copywriter and all things in between. Some writers feel more comfortable towards the scientific side, others love a creative label or feel deeply uncomfortable with high science. Personally, I believe that creativity lives everywhere. More of that later.

Types of healthcare copywriter

Medical writer
Mainly works on medical projects such as publications or monographs. Has a solid science background. Some agencies require their medical writers to have a PhD

In between the extremes are all sorts of writers in all sorts of agencies

Creative copywriter
May only work on conceptual projects. May not have a science background. Typically works in an advertising agency

Job titles vary by type of agency. What matters most is that you know where you sit in the ecosystem now, and where you're going in the future.

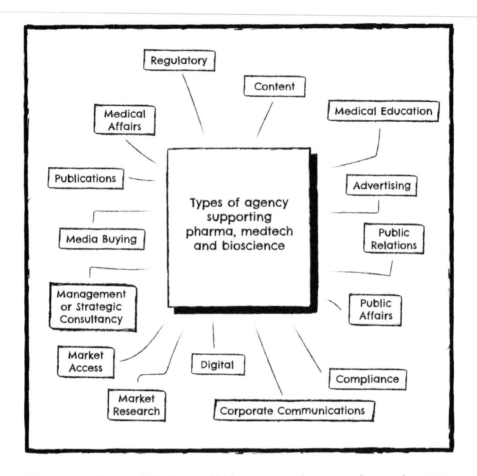

Why on earth would I share all I know so other people can become better than me?

Some people may question WHY I would write a book that can help all my competitors. I don't see it like that. I think everyone working in our industry shares my agency's purpose of making it marvellously easy to say, 'I get it'. I have never met a client who said,

"I disagree! Let's make our communication as complex as we can, so only a few can understand our messages."

Making it marvellously easy to say, 'I get it' is NOT easy. On the long road through approval, clear content is frequently ambushed and often destroyed. This makes those of us who really care, frustrated and sad because, in the end, patients suffer because of poor content. And they have enough to worry about already.

When we share a common purpose of making it marvellously easy to say, 'I get it', everyone does the right thing. As a compliance professional recently said to me,

"I want to do what's right for patients, not just what's right for compliance."

That's what I want too. I wrote this book because I want to make a genuine and lasting difference in this industry I am so proud of. I think we should all lift each other up. I hope my straight-talking book inspires you to do work that changes lives.

Why Wordbird?

I am often asked, why the Wordbird name?

If you were born after 1990, you probably have no idea that women were often referred to as 'birds' by men. As in, "I see you've got a fit new bird, Brian."

Since I was in charge of the words, Wordbird became a nickname. "Oi, Wordbird! Can you write some words for this page please?"

Now, it would be seen as an entirely inappropriate way to address a colleague, but back then it was quite normal and part of the friendly office banter.

When I came to set up my freelance business I decided to use that nickname for the business. And it has stuck. We have occasionally considered changing it to be 'more pharma'. But it is highly differentiating, so it has stayed.

What this book is not

If you are looking for any of the following, you'll need to look elsewhere:

Instructions or rules
- The opinions expressed are my own

A compliance bible
- There are others far better qualified to advise on this

CHAPTER 1

WHY does it matter?

When it comes to health, most people want to understand. The problem; what it means for their life; the treatment options; how to get the best from a medicine or device. Nobody disagrees with this. Yet a lot of health communication takes far too much brain power to make sense of. Let's dig into that a little deeper.

Brain power

I have spent my whole working life trying to make it easy for health audiences to say, 'I get it'. People can't get the most from health innovations if they don't understand them. Healthcare professionals might not make the best evidence-based decisions. Patients might suffer unnecessarily, not use the right health services, or make a mistake with their medicines.

I founded my agency, Wordbird, driven by a frustration that too much healthcare communication was baffling. Things have improved a lot, but in a world where social media-level attention spans decrease motivation to decipher content, we must constantly up our game.

To understand WHY it is so important to reduce the brain power needed to understand healthcare communications, we need to figure out how our brains process and remember information.

In 1968, Atkinson and Shiffrin proposed the Multistore Model of Memory. In this model, there are three stores:[1]

- A sensory register
- Short term, or working memory
- Long term memory

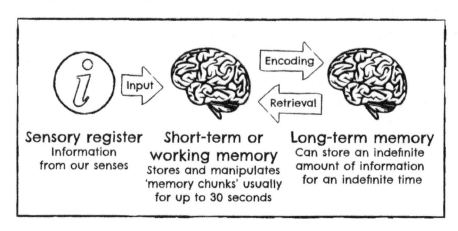

Sensory register
Information from our senses

Short-term or working memory
Stores and manipulates 'memory chunks' usually for up to 30 seconds

Long-term memory
Can store an indefinite amount of information for an indefinite time

Over the last fifty years, researchers have learned far more about these three areas of memory, so my explanation is a huge simplification.[1] The point you need to understand is that healthcare professionals, patients and carers must process and remember health information so it can be useful to them.

The job of any communicator is to make this as easy as possible. This is where cognitive load comes in.

Cognitive load is the amount of working memory it takes to process information.[2] I think of it as the *brain power* needed to take information from our senses, understand it, and remember it.

Cognitive load
The amount of working memory it takes to process information

In health communications, we often have the goal of simplicity, but we don't always understand that what we are really trying to do is reduce cognitive load, or the brain power needed 'to get it'.

It takes a HUGE amount of effort and brainpower for us to synthesise scientific information into something simple. That's because there are three Cognitive Load Cogs:[3]

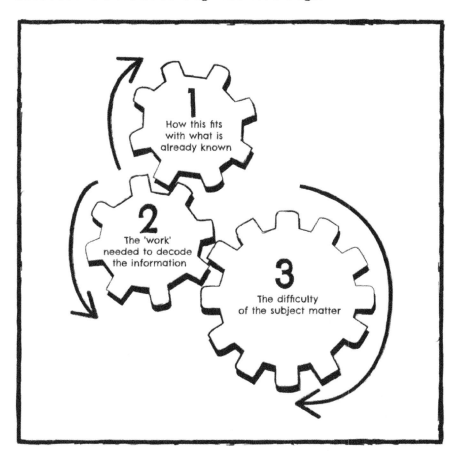

In this book, we will be looking at lots of ways to reduce cognitive load. Here are a few to get you started, related to each of the Cognitive Load Cogs. I've added the scientific terms to the table in case you want to check them out in the literature.

Type	The scientific term[3]	Make it easier by:
1. The difficulty of the subject matter	Intrinsic	Breaking information into manageable chunks and visuals Sequencing so that the bigger picture becomes clear
2. 'Work' needed to decode the information	Extraneous	Using hierarchy carefully Keeping related images and text as close as possible e.g. Label lines on a chart, rather than using a key Spelling acronyms out in full, unless you know they are very commonly used and understood by your audience Removing anything unnecessary – ruthless editing Avoiding audio and visual competition Minimising design distractions and maximising the power of white space
3. How this information fits with what the person already knows	Germaine	Showing how models fit together, e.g. Describe physiological process, then slot your solution's mode of action into the same model Being clear how ideas are connected Using analogies, patient profiles and creative concepts

Brain power self-awareness

I have often thought I have a terrible working memory. That's why I write everything down. For me, this simple act enables information to pass into my long-term memory. In fact, this is so powerful for me that I can write a shopping list, forget to take it to the supermarket and still remember most of the ingredients I need! I can see the list in my mind. I definitely don't have a photographic memory, but I do have such a strong visual memory that I can remember graphics from my university notes and drugs I worked on decades ago.

As I have investigated the science of memory, I have changed my view of my own working memory. I no longer see it as disappointing, or underperforming; I have realised that it is normal. Most people can only hold information in their working memory for about 30 seconds, and I am no different. Phew!

- How do you remember information?
- What makes it easy for you to understand the science?
- How can you bring your personal techniques into your work?

Literacy and Health Literacy

Just under half the UK population struggles to understand information that can help them manage their own health and care.[4] 7.1 million adults read at, or below, the level of a nine year old.[4]

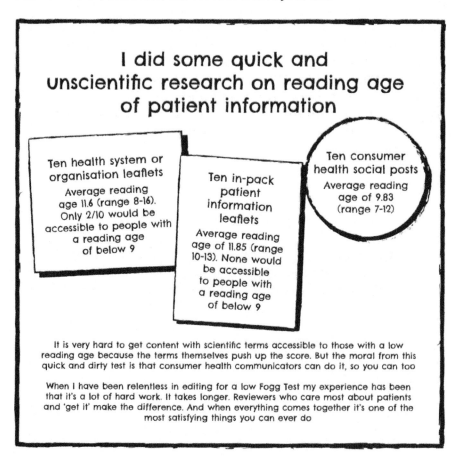

Sadly, low health literacy is linked with poor general health, increased hospital admissions, low vaccination uptake and reduced life expectancy.[4] There are divided opinions on how to take this into account when we write for patients, carers, or members of the public. Personally, I have always found The Gunning Fogg Index very helpful as a simple check of the reading age of a piece of content.

Other techniques to help:

- Use of images, infographics and films rather than lots of words
- Write short words in short sentences
- Never use a complex word when a simple one will do
- Edit ruthlessly, then get someone else to edit again

Happily, many of the things you can do to reduce cognitive load for everyone will be particularly helpful for people with low health literacy.

'I get it' moments on brainpower

At the end of each section, I have summarised the key things I hope you will remember in these 'I get it' call out boxes. That's just me trying to reduce your cognitive load. You're welcome!

- Audiences must process and remember health information so it can be useful to them
- Your job is to minimise cognitive load to make processing, encoding and retrieval easier
- Low levels of health literacy mean you need to put even more effort into health content simplification for the public
- Making it marvellously easy for others to say, 'I get it' takes a lot of brain power from you!

CHAPTER 2

7 Zones of Mastery

I started my career in healthcare communications at Luxford Advertising, based in Piccadilly, next door to Fortnum and Mason. I was overjoyed to have a job where I could use my science and develop my creativity. It was 1990. I had a new suit (with big shoulder pads) and I thought I was pretty cool mixing with the art directors and creative types. I read everything; the medical press, Campaign, books on how to write. I set out to learn all I could.

My boss was a tough taskmaster. She made me write everything multiple times. She edited ruthlessly. She quizzed me on the evidence. She encouraged me creatively and exposed me to the hard knocks of failure. She put me in front of clients from the outset. She had very high standards, and I was terrified of her! But I worked hard to impress her.

My apprenticeship was unstructured and nerve-wracking. To make yours more pleasurable, I suggest that there are 7 areas you need to gain mastery of in your first 3-10 years. What? 3-10 years? Yes, you read that right! You will certainly gain knowledge much sooner, but if it is *mastery* you want, then it will take lots of practise and lots of experience. Up for it? Let's get in the zones!

Seven Zones
of Mastery

1. Codes of practice

2. Evidence-based writing

3. Translating strategy to a content plan

4. Producing content audiences will want to engage with

5. Being a 'Creative'; the power of ideas

6. Explaining and presenting your work – how you show up

7. Developing yourself and managing yourself

CHAPTER 3

Mastery Zone 1: codes of practice

Ours is a highly regulated industry. And quite rightly so, in my opinion. Health information must be accurate. Healthcare professionals who prescribe, or recommend medicines, need to be confident they understand the potential benefits and risks. This is why there are regulations, or rules, about what we can, and can't, say or show.

Thankfully, 'the rules' are all written into various codes of practice, which vary according to what type of licence your product has, so let's start there.

Marketing authorisations and product licences

For this section, let's concentrate on medicines. The development of any new medicine takes about 12 years and costs around £1.15bn.[5] For every drug that makes it, many will have fallen by the wayside.

The diagram below shows the typical process of drug development. If you want to learn more about this process, visit the Association of The British Pharmaceutical Industry's website.

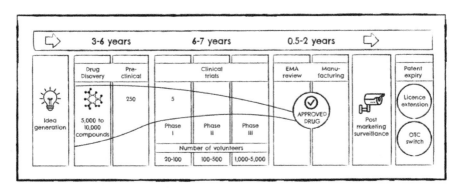

Once a company has promising phase 3 clinical trials, it can apply for a Marketing Authorisation, or MA. Marketing Authorisations are granted by regulatory bodies, like the EMA in Europe, MHRA in the UK and FDA in America.

If all goes well, a Marketing Authorisation will be granted for the drug to be marketed as a Prescription Only Medicine, or POM, and the drug will have a Licenced Indication which says what it is for.

Outside the United States, it is usually the case that Prescription Only Medicines may *only be promoted to healthcare professionals*, not to members of the public. In the UK and Europe, it is against the law to promote a Prescription Only Medicine to members of the public.

Once you know you are dealing with a Prescription Only Medicine, your promotional content will need to adhere to The Association of the British Pharmaceutical Industry (ABPI) Code of Practice if it is to appear in the UK. If you are creating core international content, you can follow the European Federation of Pharmaceutical Industries and Associations (EFPIA) Code.

Every local market will then need to approve content to their local code and laws, but the EFPIA code is very helpful at an international level. Both codes are voluntary, but since they reflect the law, they are very helpful. Anyone working in our industry should receive training on the appropriate code for them. This should be validated regularly, usually once a year. I'm not going to cover the codes here except to say you MUST know your codes, so get trained. If your employer tells you to read the code alone, that's simply not good enough. You must have training, and that needs to include examples of breaches so you can learn from previous mistakes. As you can tell, I feel pretty strongly about this because you cannot do a good job without this basic building block. In fact, I'd go as far as to say you will be incompetent. And that's a scary place to be.

I am not suggesting that everyone needs to know every detail like a lawyer, but you should:

- Know and remember the broad principles
- Know where to look things up if you are unsure — and do so frequently
- Have an expert, such as Code Clarity, to turn to when you need more help

In my agency, we run monthly sessions on the mistakes pharma companies have been accused of and how we can learn and improve based on these mistakes. These sessions don't take long and they help keep us on the rails.

Other codes of practice

Medicines that are available to buy Over The Counter (OTC) and in shops, other than pharmacies, have different legal classifications.

Each of these classifications has its own code of practice.

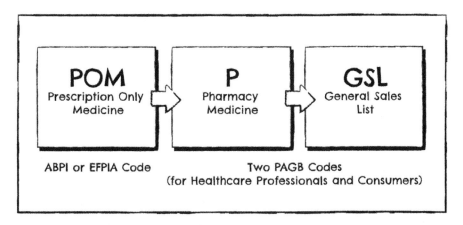

Medical devices and food supplements have different codes. The PAGB (The Consumer Healthcare Association) has codes, training, a pre-vetting service and fabulous support for those working in all areas of consumer health.

Approval processes

Whatever codes you are working to, the company promoting the medicine must have a process to check that the content is compliant. They usually involve uploading the material and marked-up references to an online portal, such as Veeva Promomats, Pepper Flow or similar.

Typically, there are 2-3 rounds of approval. Some innovators now champion a single round of review.

The people who do this job take a lot of responsibility. In theory, they could ultimately face a prison sentence if they approve and distribute materials that do not uphold the code. It's a tough gig.

In my experience, there are huge variations in the approval process. This depends on the company and individual reviewers.

Here are a few examples:

Company variations	Reviewer variations
May have requirements *in addition* to those set out in codes. Ask for Standard Operating Procedures (SOPs) beyond basic Code requirements	Personal expertise in the therapy area and expertise as a reviewer, or signatory
Costly mistakes in the past may drive an ultra-cautious, risk-averse approach	Confidence, experience or fear of dealing with potential complaints
If approving at an international level, may approve for countries with the tightest regulatory environment, or the most liberal	How they perceive their role and how they interpret the grey areas of codes
Reviewers may have autonomy, or be part of a large team with shared decision-making	Whether they are a contractor, or an employee and the support they receive from their organisation
Company passion for making a difference to patients influences their compliance culture differently	Personal thoroughness, attention to detail, and consistency with previous decisions

Avoiding spanners in the works

I'm afraid I have some bad news for you. There are some very grey areas in code interpretation. Although you will try to guess how reviewers will apply the code, you are not a mind reader.

Codes of practice exist to:

- Set standards for responsible promotion of medicines
- Reflect the overarching legal framework at a regional e.g. EU level or a national level
- Allow companies to communicate effectively with HCPs and patients so that patients can get the benefits from medicines

---

Codes are your friend, not your enemy

I have often heard people complaining that the codes are a creative straight jacket. They say that you can't do good work in such a restricted environment. They are wrong.

The people who say these things are often the ones who don't know their codes. If you don't know the rules, it's tough to do your job. You don't really know what you are doing. You don't understand what's acceptable and what is not. I used to be frustrated by the whingers. Now I feel sorry for them because they have not seen the value of investing in their own learning. You can be better than that.

I promised at the beginning that I wanted to inspire you. I appreciate that Mastery Zone 1 on codes may have left you feeling ...scared, daunted, or just a bit flat. I get it. This is not the fun bit. But stay with me. As a scientist, I think you will like Mastery Zone 2.

'I get it' moments on Codes

- Once you know the legal classification of your product, you can find out what code of practice you need to follow
- You must know your code, so you can create content to the required standard
- You need training and you must stay up to date
- There are lots of grey areas. Because you are not a mind reader, you must work closely with reviewers
- Codes are your friend, not your enemy

CHAPTER 4

Mastery Zone 2: evidence-based writing

Everything you ever write about a medicine or other health innovation must be rigorously EVIDENCE-BASED. No ifs. No buts. This is non-negotiable. And quite rightly so, because there are pros and cons with almost every health solution and we must be transparent about them all, so everyone can get the most from medicines.

I am starting with three assumptions:

1. You have a life sciences degree and understand basic biochemistry, physiology, pharmacology, anatomy and, most importantly, immunology. Almost all diseases have an immunological component and new treatments frequently have an immunological mode of action. If you don't have this, you will need the capability to teach yourself the relevant scientific concepts quickly. This is not impossible, but it demands a very high intellectual capacity.

2. You know how to read and assess a clinical paper. You'll probably have a reading order that is not linear. You'll know what makes a study robust or weak and you will be able to interpret graphs, charts and the data within a paper.

3. You will know how to research a scientific topic using Pubmed or Google Scholar. You will have a system for organising many references and an appreciation of citation techniques.

I think these are the foundation blocks of good evidence-based writing. Absence of these things does not mean you cannot become a very successful healthcare copywriter. But you do need your own strategies to overcome them.

What is evidence-based writing?

It is simply content that can be substantiated by robust scientific evidence. And you're a scientist, so surely you subscribe to that, right?

The evidence will usually be research-based and published in reputable peer-reviewed journals. We call these claims. Almost every sentence you write will have a little superscript at the end that shows exactly where your claim is from. Your claim does not need to be verbatim and can include some interpretation. For example, you might combine ideas from three papers in a single claim.

> ## Common mistakes
>
> Using the absence of something to claim a positive e.g. The paper might say 40% of people had no response to your medicine. You may not take this to mean 60% did have a response unless this is explicitly stated.
>
> Trusting sources that you receive as background to a job. Just because something has been previously approved does not necessarily mean it will be approved again.
>
> Not using a primary source. You might have a lovely review with some bold author claims you want to use. Best practice is to check the primary sources for their claim and cite all the sources. More work, but the right thing to do.
>
> Using flimsy sources such as websites that are not robustly referenced.

Pharmaceutical grade referencing

Over the years, I have interviewed many graduates who want a job as a copywriter. I always ask about attention to detail. Without fail, they earnestly tell me they have excellent referencing skills and a passion for attention to detail. But they don't know what they don't know! About three months after they start, the conversation usually goes like this:

Me: "How are you finding the referencing aspect of the job?"

Trainee copywriter: "It's so much stricter than I ever experienced before. It's another level!"

And they are right. It is another level. And so it should be. Our claims affect people's lives, so we must be evidence-based in the best possible way. I call it 'pharmaceutical grade referencing'. Pharmaceutical grade referencing prioritises guidelines, peer reviewed publications, high grade meta-analyses, 'big data', robust real world evidence and original data sources. Claims are only made when there is a statistically significant result.

The good thing is that when you get this right, it is super rewarding. And, with practise, it becomes second nature, so it's automatic. It's like driving a car. At first, driving blows your mind. You think that you will never be able to get your limbs to move in four different ways while looking, listening and figuring out which way to go, without running anyone over. After lots of practise, the effort reduces and you can enjoy the journey. I think pharmaceutical grade referencing is much the same.

Getting up the learning curve

When you first start to work on a new product, there's a lot to learn, including:

- The disease and the terminology used
- How it affects people's lives
- Who is responsible for treating it and the patient journey to treatment? For example, is it the first thing they might get, or is it used as a last resort?
- What the product offers – licenced indication, mode of action and efficacy evidence
- What side-effects are common
- How it compares to competitors
- How it is taken and if that poses any challenges

It's important that you, and everyone on your team, know the basics. Sometimes client medics will take you through the work they have already done on this to accelerate your learning. Sometimes you will be creating the slide decks they are going to use to educate others.

The quicker you can come up a learning curve, the more useful you will be to your clients and your agency. My approach to doing this is summarised below as a starter. Eventually, you will find your own way.

This is A LOT. You won't always have time for everything. Phase 1 reading is the bare minimum to have any credibility at all, and the best place to start is with the SPC.

A Summary of Product Characteristics is your best friend

Prescription Only Medicines have two important legal documents that you should read:

- Summary of Product Characteristics (Abbreviated to SPC or SmPC)
- Patient Information Leaflet (PIL)

Some also have a European Public Assessment Report (EPAR) which is a plain language summary.

The reason these documents are so useful is that they are a great starting point when you are coming up the learning curve on any medicine. I always read the SPC first because it tells me:

- Indication
- Dosage
- Who must not take it
- How it works
- Key results
- Side effects

Please note that the SPC is different to prescribing information (PI) and if your product is a long way from launch, these documents may not yet have been created.

The joy of guidelines

I love a good guideline. They tend to be excellent distillations of a therapy area, nicely describing the challenges and expert-recommended treatment pathways. When you are trying to get a helicopter view in a short space of time, they are must-read.

They will also provide you with further references to build your knowledge and usually represent an excellent source for many claims you might wish to make.

Check that the guidelines you are reading relate to the geography you are working in e.g. NICE in England and Wales, Scottish Intercollegiate Guidelines Network (SIGN), EU guidelines for Europe – you get the idea.

Supporting a trainee writer as a client

If you are reading this as a curious client, especially if you are in a more senior role, I bet you are NOT asking yourself, "how can I help the trainee writers in my communication agencies?" But why wouldn't you?

Here's a story to inspire you. When I was a Junior Writer, I supported on a big account for an antihypertensive launch. It was an intense account with a high workload and fierce deadlines. I worked my butt off on that account. The head honcho, client side, was a stickler for accuracy and quality. She was also very supportive of me. She invited me to a couple of conferences on hypertension so I could expand my understanding.

I worked on the account for three years, so that early investment in my knowledge paid dividends many times over.

You can also support agency trainees by:
- Welcoming them into the team
- Being pleasant to them – they might be the person to get you out of a fix one day
- Recognising that you probably make them very nervous
- Providing candid feedback, flagging what you would like to see more of; and less of

Documenting your investigations – Your learning curve directory

As you go up the learning curve, you will be appraising a large amount of information. You will remember some of it, but you need a simple directory to go back to for those future moments where you think, "now where did I read that?"

Because I remember 'by writing', I keep my evidence reviews and directory in a notepad, or my iPad. You might want to create a spreadsheet, or whatever suits you best. Sometimes my writers create a presentation to take our team through, so the knowledge is shared and gaps are identified. However you organise your learning curve directory and accompanying reference pack, the fact you have it can make you very valuable to your team. Remember, you don't need to remember everything, but you do need to know the source of many things!

One of the best writers I ever trained was called Sam. He was very new when he had his first expedition up the learning curve on a drug used for people who have just had a heart attack. Sam was exceptionally conscientious. He read everything. I remember him saying he thought he could actually 'do heart surgery' after all he had leaned. But he made a common mistake, one I used to make a lot. He thought he needed to know far more than he actually did. So one of the challenges is finding the Goldilocks' spot, where you know enough to do your job, without knowing so much you can't see the wood from the trees. It's a very tricky balance that comes with experience.

Learning to develop content

My favourite way to teach people to develop content is my 'Four steps to success' process.

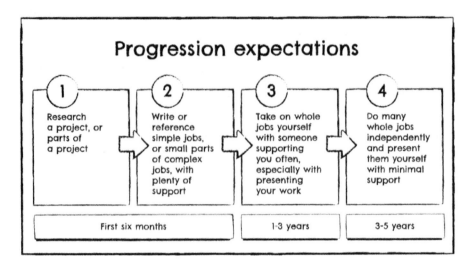

The good news is you should start making content contributions very early that your team will really value. However, you will need to work with experienced writers or editors over several years to hone your craft. Choose who you work with carefully to get the most from your experience. In Chapter 6, we will cover creating content that your audiences will want to read.

Core claims documents

Sometimes you may be asked to write a core claims document. Or you may be provided with one as a starting place. In my experience, these documents can be a mixed blessing. At worst, they are created in a vacuum without considering the audience or the strategy. At best, if they are created as a summary of core claims after a campaign has been approved, they can be more useful. Since you can look up the claims in the campaign and references on Veeva Promomats, or similar, I often advise against them and encourage clients to spend their budget on something with more value.

If core claims documents enter your world, treat with caution! Even if the claims are approved, they still need to be approvable in the context you are using them.

> ### Gender based evidence
>
> During my work with Women in Pharma, I have come to some surprising realisations that had simply never occurred to me before, even though they are patently obvious.
>
> Leaving aside genetic variations, every cell in a genetically male (XY) and female (XX) body is different. Our evolutionary biology is different. Our hormones and neurobiology are different. The rate and way we respond to diseases can be different.
>
> So why do we expect our medicines or treatment pathways to perform the same in men and women? It's a question leading scientists are asking. And I hope it's a question you will ask too.
>
> At the back of this book is an article I wrote that was published in The Medicine Maker in 2024 exploring this important topic and how the evidence needs to evolve. Let me know via LinkedIn what you think!

Modular content

Multi-channel and omnichannel, communications programmes need lots of content. In theory, chunking content into 'modules' makes it easier to create and approve lots of campaign parts that can be combined in multiple ways to meet specific customer needs.

There are lots of different ideas about modular content (sometimes called fragments) and companies define modular content very differently. It might be:

- A collective headline, claim and piece of data, or graphic
- Several screens of related content

If you are tasked with creating modular content, make sure you know how YOUR client defines modular content, the referencing requirements, how modules must fit together, and the job code requirements.

Job codes

Job codes appear on every material as standard. They are a great way for clients to track what's been approved and when it needs to be reapproved, which is required for Code compliance.

Approval systems usually generate job numbers as part of setting up a job and they are normally different for medical and commercial activities.

How will AI change things?

AI will change all our jobs in ways that we haven't even thought of yet. ChatGPT predicts that:

AI will transform healthcare communication for pharma by tailoring content to individual patients, automating personalised messaging, and facilitating efficient doctor-patient interactions, ultimately improving overall healthcare experiences.

At the time of writing (March 2024) a paid-for, up-to-date version of ChatGPT should be part of your toolkit. If you ask it to provide a referenced document, it will do so, BUT:

- Poorly prompted copy is generally poor copy. The knack is in multiple re-prompts to fine-tune your request and the output. You need to be quite crafty to get a solid 'first draft'
- You must always check back to the primary references. Referencing quality is not **yet** accurate enough; the references might not exist or be poor quality
- You still need to work hard to ensure copy is code compliant and on-strategy
- As with all AI content generation tools, copyright legislation lags behind what is possible, so be very careful about inadvertently breaking copyright law
- Badly edited (or unedited) AI-generated copy can intuitively feel a little 'odd' to readers and can be 'off brand'
- There's an art to asking for what we need. This is where the steep learning and continued effort is needed now

AI is learning all the time, so treat it like a learner. It needs lots of help right now, but it is an essential time saver so use it wisely.

> **Use the TIPTOE acronym to give ChatGPT specific instructions:**
>
> Task – Tell it what you need
>
> Information – Give it what it needs to do the job. Upload any documents.
>
> Persona – Who do you want it to write as; a doctor, a friendly nurse, a key opinion leader
>
> Tone – Tell it what you want e.g. Mix of short and long sentences, businesslike, in the tone of someone famous
>
> Output – Tell it what format you need it in e.g. Word
>
> Edit – Check and edit the output forensically.

As this area develops, new tools will arrive to help create the content we need. Staying up to date will be an essential part of your job. You can add value to your agency and clients by taking a lead and sharing your knowledge.

If you are a lover of science and clarity, then this chapter will have been very reassuring. The qualification you have worked so hard for can be put to exceptionally good use. And you will be helping healthcare professionals, clients and patients. You should expect lots of support from your team through the early years until you become perfectly competent at producing evidence-based content.

'I get it' moments on evidence-based writing

- Everything you ever write about a medicine or other health innovation must be rigorously EVIDENCE-BASED
- Almost every sentence you write will have a little superscript at the end that shows exactly where your claim is from
- You need to develop your own techniques for coming up a learning curve and documenting your sources carefully so you know where to find every potential claim in a Learning Curve Directory
- Know your clients' requirements for modular content – they vary
- AI will change everything, but humans will still be needed to maximise the value of the AI – stay ahead so you can lead the knowledge sharing in this area

CHAPTER 5

Mastery Zone 3: translating strategy to a content plan

Now things start to get juicy! Before you can create any content, you MUST know what the strategy is for the brand and for the piece of content you are writing. So let's start with strategy. I LOVE communication strategy. Even when strategy has not been 'officially' part of my role, I was magnetically attracted to it. I used to work with a brilliant strategist called John. I often acted as his sounding board, and John got me hooked on strategy. Strategy demands a huge amount of brain power, but John taught me how it could be so much fun.

What even is strategy?

When I worked for the stop smoking charity, QUIT, we were part of a coalition of organisations whose shared purpose was to reduce the health effects of smoking. We were united in our efforts to campaign for a ban on cigarette advertising and smoking in public places. Of course, now it seems incredible that you could smoke anywhere, even on a plane. Revolting! I attended a great training at what was then called the Health Education Authority.

They explained that strategy was a military term. When leaders of ancient civilisations faced a battlefield, they needed to win, but how? What position would they choose? How would they deploy their troops? Would they use surprise, trickery, or play a waiting game?

Once the generals had decided their strategy, it was enacted by the troops applying their instructions and training. These were tactics. Tactics win battles. Strategy wins wars.

These days, strategy is used in lots of different ways. This can be very confusing. The strategy that we are most interested in is communication strategy.

Communications strategy

All brands need a communication strategy. For now, here are some thoughts on what you should be looking for and asking about.

There are lots of different models of communication strategy. Agencies and industry use many variations. Some are very complex and hard to work with at a practical level. The best are relentlessly simple. You need to know:

- Who is your audience?
- What are their challenges and ambitions?
- How does your solution help them?
- What do they think, feel and do now?
- How do we want our communication to change what they think, feel and do?
- The communication strategy for the brand overall and, for tactical briefs, what part of the strategy the tactic is addressing

This information should be included in the brief you will receive. The brief might be written by:

- A strategist
- An account manager or account director
- A client

All our communication is trying to bring about some kind of behaviour change, for example persuading the audience to:

- Notice unmet needs
- Re-evaluate something that is done by habit
- Assess a new solution
- See an old problem in a new light
- Stop doing one thing and start doing something else
- Do more of something they are already doing
- Engage with a representative, some online content or attend an event
- Discuss something with their colleagues

> ### 'Types of strategy'
>
> Commercial Strategy – The choices a company makes about where it is going to operate and how it is going to be successful
>
> Other strategies sit beneath commercial strategy, such as:
>
> - Brand strategy
> - Pricing strategy
> - Market access strategy
> - Procurement strategy
> - Communication strategy
> - Staffing strategy

> **'What can happen when you don't start with strategy?**
>
> Everyone has different ideas about what needs to be achieved – the team is not united.
>
> The development of tactics goes round in circles, taking longer than anticipated and becoming frustrating for all.
>
> It's like an army that does not have an overall strategy – everyone does what they think is best, but there is no overall agreement, so actions can be in conflict and the army becomes its own worst enemy.
>
> However, I never regret demanding high standards in a brief and neither should you.

A content plan is a blueprint for behaviour change

Being the top geek that I am, I find assembling the evidence in a way that can best serve the audience, very enjoyable and satisfying. If you have been conscientious in creating your learning curve directory, you will have a fantastic evidence source that will feed into your content plans.

Healthcare professionals are exceptionally busy people. The demands on them are huge. They are also humans on social media and subject to the dwindling attention spans that affect us all.

Whatever precious time companies get to engage with them must be spent in a way that:

- Captures and holds their attention
- Gives them something valuable
- Requires minimum brain power to understand and remember
- Changes their behaviour

Humans are wired to encode information as stories. As our cave dwelling ancestors sat round the fire, they told stories that were remembered and turned into visuals on their walls. We can tap into that primal instinct by bringing our evidence together in a way that tells a story.

The best stories have a beginning, a middle and an end. So our most basic story for a module might be just that. On the next page there's a fictitious example for a short efficacy story content plan.

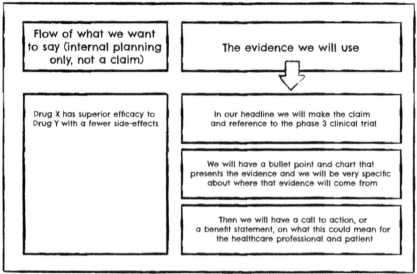

This is how it might look

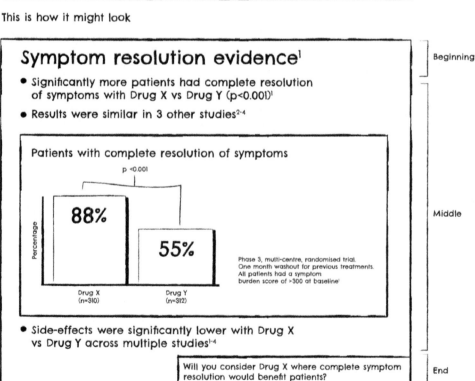

Here's an example for a content plan (or story) for a typical visual aid to support an in-person or virtual representative meeting.

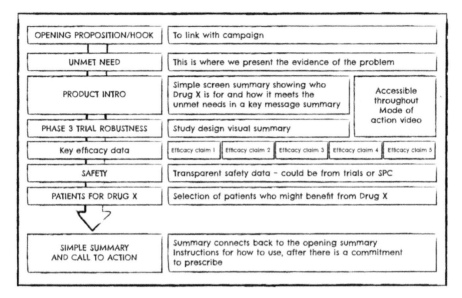

I have tried lots of formats and always return to this one for simple jobs because:

- It is clear and easy to follow
- Everyone can see the big picture and the planned detail/evidence
- It is easy to evaluate whether the proposed content will deliver the strategy
- Everyone can judge whether the plan has Code compliance 'baked in'

The general principle is the same for customer journey content, websites and interactive site maps – they are just larger and more complex.

Get everyone on board with the content plan early

Successful and smooth-running jobs start with everyone agreeing a plan. That's your agency team and everyone who will be involved on the client side. The jargon for this group is 'stakeholders'.

Spending time sharing and discussing your content plan is very important. If anyone disagrees, or there are mistakes or misunderstandings, you can make changes to the plan.

Your wider team may also know of even better data you can use, pitfalls to avoid, and you may flush out any personal preferences.

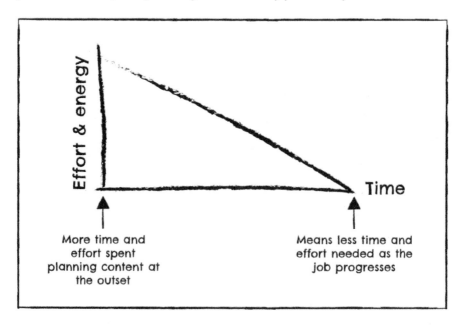

Content plans are your springboard to success. They are the rainbow road between strategy and content. Done well, they will make everyone's life easier. Do not neglect them, even for the simplest job. Many a simple job has turned into a costly and painful nightmare because it lacked a brief and a content plan. You won't believe me on this until it happens to you. After that I hope you will become a content plan enthusiast too!

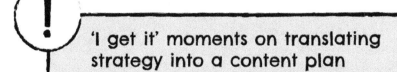

'I get it' moments on translating strategy into a content plan

- Be clear on the communication strategy and the brief
- The directory you created when coming up the learning curve is your content plan evidence source
- Content plans are a blueprint for behaviour change
- Content plans tell stories; they have a beginning, a middle and an end
- Share your plan at the outset and ensure everyone's on board

CHAPTER 6

Mastery Zone 4: producing content audiences will want to engage with

I hope you are enjoying this book. I have worked hard to write it with you in mind. To see things through your eyes. To hear a specific voice in my head as I write. To make it easy for you to read and process, so you get the maximum value with the minimum cognitive load. And now I am going to share how you can do exactly the same for your health audiences. Let's enter Mastery Zone 4.

'Write from wrong'

I developed 'Write from wrong' as a north star for trainee writers many years ago. Whenever I ask the best Wordbird writing alumni what the most useful thing they learned while under my wing, 'Write from wrong' is always pivotal.

Write from wrong

1. Know your audience
2. Have an idea
3. Make a plan
4. Know your ending
5. Use the right number of words
6. Keep it simple
7. Make it interesting
8. Write visually
9. Leave out more than you put in

> I use the term 'content' broadly. Examples of content you might be creating include:
>
> - Websites
> - Apps
> - Emails
> - Social media posts
> - Video scripts
> - Mode of action or explainer videos/animations
> - Disease awareness content
> - Modules
> - Medical decks
> - Visual aids
> - Summary leaflets
> - Patient content
> - Carer content
> - Training materials
> - Brand guides
> - Campaign implementation guides
> - Press releases
> - Manuscripts
> - Regulatory documents

1. Know your audience

I like to think of myself as a student of human nature. When I was in my teens my life was DULL. Not much TV, no mobiles or social media. Money was tight, so I filled the interminable hours with reading. I escaped my dreary reality through Agatha Christie murder mystery books. One of her most famous characters, Miss Marple, was also an observer of human nature. Miss Marple's superpower was noticing the little things and drawing parallels with similar situations she had encountered elsewhere. You can use a similar technique to get to know your audiences.

Let's start with patients. At some point in your life, you have been ill. You have been a patient yourself. You might have had a health scare, or know someone who has.

You, or a friend or relative, might have a chronic condition, or been through treatment for a life-threatening disease.

You have almost certainly been to a GP or visited a pharmacy. There's a good chance you have seen a nurse, been inside a hospital or have a close family member with experience of health services.

You have lots of 'lived experience' to draw on. You can travel into your own mind and notice how you felt when you were ill. What it was like to prepare for a consultation with a healthcare professional? How were you questioned? Could you tell your story? How did you prepare in the waiting room?

I'm hoping you have a great imagination. Let's try a three-part thought experiment.

1. Imagine how it would feel to get a diagnosis that would completely change your life
2. Imagine how your weekly hospital visits would fit into your life
3. Imagine a close relative is going to die

What did you feel? When I do thought experiment 1, I feel devastated, frustrated and driven to find out more.

The idea of weekly hospital visits is stressful to me: how would I fit it all in? What about transport? Could I drive or work? How would I get money to live? I feel the stress hormones cortisol and adrenaline flooding my system. The idea of my husband, or one of my sons, having a disease that will kill them is almost too painful to imagine. Just the thought changes my body chemistry. It immediately makes me feel like crying and I enter 'crisis mode'.

Empathy[6]

- Vicariously experiencing another person's emotions
- Deliberately experiencing another person's perspective in order to understand their thoughts and feelings
- A desire to improve another person's welfare

Since you are a scientist, you'll be fascinated to learn that there's a link between imagination, empathy and memory.[6]

Research techniques to find out more about patients and carers

- Social listening
- Patient organisation websites, YouTube and social media
- Talking to people with the condition (respecting your confidentiality contractual obligations and Code considerations)
- Use tools like Health Unlocked or other surveys
- PubMed search on patient perspectives and quality of life studies
- Professional body publications e.g. Royal College website
- Patient journeys
- Market research with patients

Those who write well for patients or carers have great empathy, but they also research their audience thoroughly. My favourite way of deeply understanding my audience is to follow relevant patient organisations on Instagram. I look at Insta every day so I pick up the hot topics and save the posts that inspire me. It's a super quick way to stay in the know so I can be an expert advisor.

Stepping into healthcare professional shoes is similar, but it is more dangerous to make assumptions about how healthcare professionals feel about their patients and speciality. For example, you might imagine that giving a cancer diagnosis is emotional for doctors. For some it is, but practise makes it easier. Some oncologists deliberately detach from the emotion and drama of their patients' lives so they can have a clear head for decisions. Within each therapeutic area, there are usually different 'types' of healthcare professionals with different attitudes, behaviours and treatment approaches.

Companies usually conduct segmentation market research to understand these groups better. Segmentation can be very different by therapy area.

Examples of segments

- Pioneers
- Workload survivors
- Guideline followers
- Patient-champions
- Passionate educators
- Altruistic leaders
- Bombastic autocrats
- Confidence seekers
- Technicians

If you want to feel confident developing communications for healthcare professionals, my advice is to get to know them in your personal life. If you have healthcare professional friends or contacts, meet up. Be curious about their working lives. Can you set up a group chat where you can ask them questions?

Think about how you can build your network in a way that gives you access to a range of healthcare professionals who might be open to helping you. I must stress the importance of acting within your contract and Code. If you don't know how to interact with healthcare professionals in a way that won't get you into trouble, ask for training. Never risk a Code or contractual breach.

2. Have an idea

You need to attract people to read, watch, listen, discuss, or attend. And I have news for you. Information alone is rarely enough to do this.

Let me say that again. Information alone is usually not enough. Is that a surprise to you? One of the greatest advertising minds of all time, Bill Bernbach, wisely said;

"Our job is to bring the dead facts to life."

Bernbach was talking about consumer goods, but I think it is even more important in our industry. We have a lot of dead facts.

Our information needs to be packaged in an interesting way because it REALLY matters that it gets the attention it needs. At the extreme, it might be a matter of life and death.

Ideas are a great way to connect with people and get your brand, or content, noticed. In the 7th Zone of Mastery I'll share more about ideas, but for now, let's think about ideas in their simplest form and take the example of a disease awareness social post.

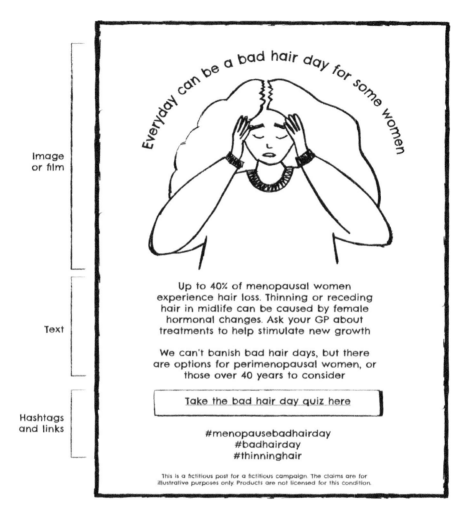

Imagine we want perimenopausal women to know that there is a prescription treatment available for hair loss. We could just provide some facts, or we could weave an idea throughout the post. It's even better if it has an emotional connection. There are three places an idea can live in a social post:

This post could be part of a wider campaign where the 'bad hair day' idea lives in other forms. When it comes to more clinical information, we could have an overarching idea for a medical slide deck that wraps the data in an engaging theme. For example, 'Weighing up the evidence in breast cancer', or 'Rethinking heart disease', or 'Below the surface in eczema'. Medical journals also use ideas and themes in headlines to grab a reader's attention. A favourite of mine is, 'Shall we stay or shall we switch?' in an ophthalmology journal, referencing an old song by The Clash.

3. Make a plan

In Mastery Zone 3, I explained how to translate strategy into a content plan and the value of doing this for EVERY SINGLE JOB!

A clear plan is an essential foundation for producing content audiences will want to engage with. Without a plan, your content might be jumbled, or require too much brain power to decipher.

You should also remember that plans change. When I was a rookie writer, I used to get INFURIATED when clients changed their minds and plans changed. I simply could not understand why they didn't decide at the beginning and stick to the plan. With experience, I have learned that the first plan is 'a theory'. When people agree to the plan, they are agreeing 'in principle'. The first draft is an experiment to test the theory. You and your team might see:

- Something that doesn't quite work
- A way to do something better
- An opportunity to bring in a different angle
- A gap in the argument

When content changes, I always amend the plan so I am clear on the big picture – or the 'new theory'. If changes unintentionally affect the strategy, you can play a valuable role by noticing and pointing it out.

A content plan is also very useful for planning your time and celebrating progress. I am a big fan of maximising the benefits of regular dopamine hits when I have a little win. Ticking off progress on a content plan is perfect for this. When you know how far through a job you are, you can update and reassure your team, or let them know if you need help to meet a deadline.

Plans are soooooooo useful. I never leave home without one!

4. Know your ending

A good story always has a good ending. It's the same with content. Something must happen as a result of your communication. When you know your ending at the outset, you can produce a streamlined flow that ends exactly where you want it to.

Here's an example.

I'm writing an email to offer dentists an online meeting to hear about some new clinical data on a toothpaste. The meeting will be with a representative from the company. Let's call the company Big Dental and the toothpaste Enamel-XP.

I need to build a good case to persuade dentists to give up their valuable time to hear about Enamel-XP. And then I need to get them to commit to a meeting.

After I have been very clear why dentists would want to see the new data, my ending would ask for what I want.

Please use the online calendar below to arrange a time when your Big Dental representative can present this important new data. It could make a significant difference to your patients with gingivitis.

The purest example is in an advertisement. The ending, often the strapline under the logo, should be a perfect end to the communication.

5. Use the right number of words

Writing for school or university is very different to being a professional writer in any industry. At university, you probably used lots of 'filler words' to get your dissertation to the required word count. There were no prizes for 'writing short'.

> **Filler words to wave goodbye to**
>
> Unless you are writing manuscripts, you will rarely need:
>
> - Therefore
> - However
> - A number of reasons
> - Considering
> - Nevertheless
> - Conversely
> - Hence
> - Nothwithstanding

In healthcare communications, brevity is EVERYTHING. Healthcare professional audiences have very little time, and patients need simplicity.

The right number of words is usually the fewest words you can possibly use to convey your message in a compliant way, in the desired tone of voice.

Here's an example. Which of these options decreases cognitive load for you?

Drug A outperformed Drug B in all primary and secondary measures of efficacy ($p<0.001$). Conversely, Drug B was worse on efficacy outcomes. [22 words]

Drug A was more effective than Drug B in all efficacy parameters (p<0.001) [13 words]

When I started out, I found it infuriating that I was always told to write shorter. Be more punchy. Didn't they appreciate all the effort I had put in to hone this text? Of course, I was wrong and needed to learn to 'write short'.

My top tip for 'writing short' is to challenge yourself on word-count, aiming to half your word-count from a draft one. If your initial word-count is 50, try to get it to 25. It will seem impossible at first, like driving a car. But you will get there. With practise, I believe you can be a sought-after writer or editor, who edits for brevity without even thinking about it.

In writing this book, I have not written particularly short. But I have used the right number of words. That is because I need to hold your attention. My chatty tone of voice needs more words, and that's OK for a book or an article.

When you are writing copy to go with an image, in an advertisement, for example, you can usually use even fewer words. That's because the two work together to communicate your message explicitly and implicitly.

Deploy your word-count with wisdom and intention. The number of words you use should not be an accident.

> **Ideal average sentence length**
>
> "Most experts would agree that clear writing should have an average sentence length of 15-20 words."
>
> The Plain English Campaign

6. Keep it simple

I hope my previous chapters on cognitive load and health literacy have convinced you of the need to keep everything simple. Here's a reminder:

- Audiences must process and remember health information so it can be useful to them
- Your job is to minimise cognitive load to make processing, encoding and retrieval easier
- Low levels of health literacy mean you need to put even more effort into health content simplification for the public
- Making it marvellously easy for others to say, 'I get it' takes a lot of brain power from you

Here are some ways you can minimise the brain power needed to understand your content, remembering the three Cognitive Cogs:

1. The difficulty of the subject matter
2. The 'work' needed to decode the information
3. How this information fits with what the person already knows

- Break information into manageable chunks and visuals
- Sequence carefully so that the bigger picture is clear
- Using hierarchy carefully

- Keep related images and text as close as possible e.g. label lines on a chart, rather than using a key
- Spell acronyms out in full, unless you know that they are very commonly used and understood by your audience
- Remove anything unnecessary – ruthless editing
- Avoid audio and visual competition
- Minimise design distractions and maximise the power of white space
- Show how models fit together e.g. Describe a physiological process, then slot your drug's mode of action into the same model
- Be clear how ideas are connected
- Use analogies and creative concepts

Short sentences and readability

Do you sometimes read a book and suddenly realise you have not taken anything in? You might go back and re-read a chapter again because of this. Maybe you weren't concentrating because you were tired, multi-tasking, the story was dull, or the language too complex.

As a content creator, you have no control over whether your reader is tired. You can assume they WILL be distracted, but you have zero control over that either. The thing you can control is how interesting and readable your content is.

Let's start with readability. Long sentences are a major barrier to readability. When I edit other people's writing, shortening sentences is transformational. I have noticed that many people have a resistance to very short sentences. Like this one. Maybe that stems from our education system, where complex, multi-clause sentences are prized. But very short sentences have incredible power. I urge you to recognise any inner resistance to short sentences and go beyond it.

Short sentences, combined with longer sentences, create rhythm in writing. Rhythm makes text more pleasant to read. I hear your inner scientist screaming, is that really true? Hello inner scientist!

Let me persuade you with this beautiful demonstration from the San José State University Writing Center.

"Rhythm is how writing sounds and how sentences and ideas are connected. Monotonous writing is the absence of rhythm, as shown in the example below.[7]

This sentence has five words. Here are five more words. Five-word sentences are fine. But several together become monotonous. Listen to what is happening. The writing is getting boring. The sound of it drones. It's like a stuck record. The ear demands some variety."

See how the same author adds rhythm to their writing.

"Sentence variety creates rhythm. Having the same length and/or type of sentences repeatedly creates monotony and makes the writing difficult for the reader to get through. Conversely, variety engages the reader. It captures the eye and makes text easier to read. Variety can be created by sentence length, sentence complexity, and intentional punctuation choices."[7]

UX (User Experience) companies use big data to analyse the performance of ecommerce sites. In addition to sentence length, design factors also affect readability and subsequent purchase.[8]
- Text line length of 80 characters or less
- Line height
- Paragraph spacing
- Word spacing
- Letter spacing

Jargon and acronyms

I often feel I wage a one-woman crusade against the use of jargon and acronyms. But why do I care so much?

If you subscribe to the view that we should be aiming to make it marvellously easy to say, 'I get it', then you will agree that we should remove barriers to processing information and decrease the cognitive load (brain power) demanded from our audiences.

Using a more complex word, such as 'utilise', instead of 'use', demands a tiny bit more from your audience. Although small and insignificant on its own, I would argue that lots of these small demands on our audiences' brain power add up.

Let's take a step back to consider the opportunity to exploit 'the aggregation of marginal gains'. This is the philosophy of searching for a tiny marginal improvement in everything you do.[9]

This term was made famous by the Performance Director of British Cycling, Dave Brailsford. When he joined in 2003, British Cycling had endured almost 100 years of mediocrity. They had never won an Olympic gold medal or The Tour de France.[9]

Dave Brailsford optimised everything from the obvious (cycle design) to the obscure (massage gel for faster muscle recovery). They tested everything to find as many 1% gains as they could. Hundreds of small improvements accumulated and soon British Cycling dominated at the Olympics and enjoyed consistent success in The Tour de France.

I believe there is an opportunity to use 'the aggregation of marginal gains' in health communication content too. The first place to start is by reducing jargon and spelling out acronyms; often at every mention. When everyone is on board, relentless simplification can make a big difference.

Why do we love jargon so much?

Here is my personal, non-evidence-based theory.

Pharma is jargontastic. People don't appear to notice that within corporate pharma a special language has appeared. Whenever new graduates come to client meetings, I warn them that it might be hard to figure out what people are talking about.

Pharma folk seem blissfully unaware how hard it can be for outsiders to decode discussions; 'pending multidisciplinary, stakeholder decisions.' 'Waiting for MLR approval of the PI and IIT.' Or 'aligning on a POA for the walled garden'.

I believe this language creates a fraternal feeling of belonging, which people find comforting. In an industry where restructure is almost continual and job security often shaky, comfort is completely understandable.

But jargon is infectious! When we spend a lot of time with jargonistas we start to speak fluent jargon too. It is so hard to resist.

In my opinion, those who show up intentionally, with a simplicity mindset, get the best content. But I do understand how corporate culture and compliance can make this something of a quest.

The Plain English Campaign

If you are interested in learning more about jargon-free communications, The Plain English Campaign is a great place to start (plainenglish.co.uk).

This organisation campaigns against gobbledygook, jargon and misleading public information. Their guides, based on experience with thousands of documents, are well worth a read.

Language is always evolving

As lexicographer and etymologist, Susie Dent, often points out, language never stands still. Today's slang becomes tomorrow's mainstream. Fashions and tastes in words change. So today's jargon might become tomorrow's everyday chat!

Word of the Year

In December each year The Oxford University press publishes its Word of the Year.

2023 – Rizz

'Style charm or attractiveness'

2022 – 'Goblin mode'

'Unapologetically self-indulgent, lazy, slovenly or greedy behaviour.'

If you are interested in language trends like this, follow Susie Dent on social media.

A great example are those Shakespearean phrases we now use every day:
- Love is blind
- A wild goose chase
- Make your hair stand on end
- The world is your oyster

Your job is to keep your finger on the pulse, so your work is always relevant to the intended audience.

7. Make it interesting

This is not quite the same thing as having an idea, although they are closely related and another way to bring dead facts to life.

Interest often comes from bringing the outside in. What I mean by that is taking some knowledge, information, insight, scientific concept or popular idea and using it to make your content more relatable, informative, attractive, creative or 'new'.

> **The difference between interest and insights**
>
> A hook for interest is what makes people take notice
>
> An insight is what makes people care – and it can also be what makes them take notice

Making things interesting is demanding. It requires that you go outside your day job and show interest in the world. A brief is just the start. 'Interesting' means you add value by bringing an extra dimension. Here's an example. My team was working on some virtual meeting in a box content. We knew what we wanted to convey, but it was unlikely to entice doctors to sign up for the meeting. Until we 'looked outside' we struggled to come up with anything beyond 'case studies'. In truth, our initial thoughts were dull.

After some deep thought, we hit on the idea of starting with an idea from the science of behavioural economics. Then we wrapped the meeting in a box in that theme. Now, this WAS interesting to doctors because it connected two things they were interested in, in a new way that they hadn't seen before.

The idea came from a talk I had been to several years before by Paul Dolan, Professor of Behavioural Science at The London School of Economics. My brain had stored away the stimulus and remembered it in a way that was useful years later.

> ### Sources of outside stimuli
>
> - Podcasts – for science, you can't beat 'Huberman Lab' and business, Simon Sinek's 'A Bit of Optimism' has great guests, who you can follow up on after listening
> - Art and design exhibitions
> - Talks – check out Eventbright and LinkedIn lives
> - Follow patient organisations on social media
> - Read business books – often the first few chapters tell you all you need to know
> - Be knowledgeable about popular culture, maybe through TV and social media
> - Follow science journals online – usually they have a free weekly email with headline news. I follow BMJ and JAMA and get all sorts of ideas from their weekly emails

When I was mum to young children, I took them to all sorts of exhibitions and events for children. At that time, I happened to be working on several consumer medicines for children. Lots of the content we created at that time was directly inspired by my lived experience of life as a mum.

Sometimes interest is 'hidden' within your source scientific content. The introduction to papers often explains a problem, or refers to a scientific insight that can be your hook. You might also gain insights from market research that, combined with something else, make your content much more interesting.

It's always important to 'test' your ideas for making something interesting. This could be by talking with the medical team on the account, or with customers through an advisory board or market research. Even better, go to congresses and attend symposia. Listening to customers will often give you ideas on what's interesting to them. It might be very different to what YOU find interesting!

8. Write visually

Here are some examples of visual content you might be creating:

- Mode of action animations or diagrams
- Graphs and charts
- Explainer animations or graphics
- Brand concepts
- Infographics
- Exhibitions and congresses
- Social media posts

My advice here is very simple. Figure out what you want to say in words, then, WHEREVER POSSIBLE, turn it into a picture.

Have a go at doing this yourself using pen and paper, or an iPad. Draw your idea or diagram. Yes, draw it. Don't worry that it's not perfect. Do it quickly. This is not an exam. It's a process to get to a brilliant result. Take a photo of your best version and make it part of your copy document. You could even upload it to ChatGPT and ask it for refinements.

> ## Overcoming your inner resistance to drawing
>
> I have rarely trained anyone who hasn't felt inner resistance to drawing their ideas for visual communication.
>
> Like you, they'll procrastinate and create all sorts of excuses not to give it a go. I hear you. Recognise the inner resistance calling you to stay in your comfort zone.
>
> Acknowledge it. Then go beyond it. That's your growth zone. The magic zone. It's where the best work will happen. There is no need to be scared.

Next step, work with a designer or art director. Share your ambition for the communication. What are you trying to achieve? Explain how far you have got on your own. Show them your scribble(s). Ask how they would make it better. Do lots of drawings together. Quiz ChatGPT together. Chances are, they will have an even better idea. They might be thinking laterally and lead you to an even better place. Remember that this is their area of expertise. They will have trained in visual communication for several years, just like you have trained in science. You need to learn from them, so listen to their wisdom. Ask for their advice. Once you have some fabulous thinking, they will be able to create a professional rendition to share with clients.

What's the difference between a graphic designer, an art director and an artworker?

A designer communicates ideas and content through images, layout, and typography, often following brand guidelines. There are many specialities of designer that you might work with.

An art director works at a more conceptual level, overseeing visual content, creating new visual identities, commissioning illustration, animation and directing photography shoots.

An artworker takes the 'rough' designs and prepares them for the specific media they will be used in, for example, 'retina quality' for iPad, or sized correctly for printing. Digital and print content is made differently, using different colour systems.

The creative director leads on ideas generation, manages a creative department and oversees everything to ensure that quality is always tip top. Here's what award-winning Creative Director Lawrence Clift has to say on the power of art directors and copywriters working together:

"A creative idea is a whole made up of the visual and the words. As a writer, the more you can develop your art direction skills and an understanding of the visual side of things, the more you can come up with a whole, rounded idea. And it's the same for an art director. An art director who doesn't have a good understanding of copy and how that works will only be capable of half the big idea. In a magical partnership, a writer often has the idea for a visual and the art director for the headline. Writers should think beyond copy. The more you can develop both sides of creative, the more your ideas will fly."

Your agency might not be set up to work this way. This process of working together might need to come from you. If you want to write visually, you will find it hard to do alone in the early stages of your career, so it's worth making the effort to ask for opportunities to work with a designer or art director. I appreciate that this might feel hard to do. Here's what you could say:

"I have been thinking about the best way to help our audience understand [_____]. I have some visual ideas that will make it easier for people to process and remember. I've taken these as far as I can on my own. Can I spend some time working with [_____] to make them even better?"

In our industry, we are blessed with lots of data and concepts that we can visualise beautifully. Our beautiful visualisation can play a big part in making it marvellously easy to say, 'I get it'. If you want some training on this, David McCandless' Information is Beautiful website has details of his workshops, which you can join for a relatively low cost. Ask your agency to cover this cost as part of your continuing professional development (CPD). Don't forget that, although a bit clunky now (March 2024) AI is transforming this process at a breathtaking pace. Stay up to date.

9. Leave out more than you put in

When a movie is made, the director shoots far more than will ever end up on the silver screen. Only the very best takes make it into the film. The rest is discarded. It's the same with creating healthcare content. You must always leave out more than you put in. Sometimes that's hard. You have so much good stuff to convey. But there is a danger. The more you add, the less clear things become for your audience. They are only human; busy, distracted, creatures of habit.

In my experience, market research usually tells us to take content out. Inexperienced clients and agency staff have a strong tendency to ignore this request, cramming in as much as possible, covering every available space. The most experienced and successful people in our industry know that less is always more. And it makes sense. Reducing cognitive load requires ruthless brevity.

Producing health content that people want to read isn't easy

There's so much to remember. So many things to consider. I used to feel like my head would fall off trying to bring it all together! Don't worry, my head is still attached and yours will be too. Get into the habit of using 'Write from Wrong'. It will eventually make your life easier. *Eventually*. Stick with it my friend. You can do this.

No cherry picking!

I love cherries! Sour, sweet, in cake or a dessert. Delicious! But in our work world, we must show fair balance. We cannot cherry pick data that is unrepresentative of the whole.

There are some things we cannot leave out. Check your codes. Don't leave out the wrong stuff.

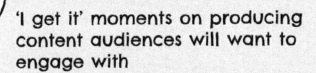

'I get it' moments on producing content audiences will want to engage with

- Know your audience – research them, develop empathy and be curious
- Bring the dead facts to life with ideas
- Have a clear plan and stay flexible until the end of the job
- Know your ending and be clear on what should happen as a result of the communication
- The right number of words is usually as short as you can manage, but not always
- Making content interesting demands that you go the extra mile to look 'outside' to find out what's hot in patient and HCPs' worlds – or bring them relevant ideas from outside their world
- Learn to write visually by working with a designer or art director
- Leave out more than you put in

CHAPTER 7

Mastery Zone 5: being a 'Creative'; the power of ideas

You are a 'scientist', right? Wrong! You are a 'scientist' who is also a 'creative'. How do I know this? Because all science is rooted in creativity. Scientists solve the problems of the world. Scientists have a creative idea. They call it a hypothesis. They test their hypothesis and create a new one if the original one is disproven. I know that if you are interested in science, you must also be creative. Maybe your creativity is close to the surface. Maybe it's deeply buried. Let's unlock your creative inner self.

How do we lose our creative identity?

We all start off with belief in our creative abilities. As children, most of us draw, paint and play imaginary games. We are relentless curiosity machines. We ask SO many questions. Adults encourage us to be creative. They praise our artistic endeavours, encourage play and experimentation.

As we reach our teens, everything changes. We change. The expectations of us change. Something inexplicable happens. Some of us come out of our teens 'labelled' creative. And some do not. Some non-creatives are 'labelled' academic. If you studied science at university, I bet your proud parents think of you as academic, and there is nothing wrong with that. But we can be more than one thing. If we don't have the creative 'label', we might feel we can't be creative, especially at work.

Reclaim your creative identity

Like most things, it starts with intention. Most people have a creative aspect to their home life.

Do you enjoy:
- Reading
- Theatre
- Film
- Gaming
- Music
- Art and design exhibitions
- Crafting
- Entertaining
- Fashion and retail
- Hair and beauty
- Podcasts
- Writing for pleasure
- Magazines or photography
- Interior design
- Playing with children in your life
- Sport or exercise

All of these can have an element of creativity. Even armchair sports people have ideas about what the manager should have done differently. They have imagined a different reality, which is creative.

When I interview people, I like to ask about creativity and culture. What are they reading, who do they follow on social media, what's creative about them? I believe everyone is creative. Including you. Banish your Imposter Syndrome. There is no basis for it. Let's move on.

How the geeky Human Biologist overcame her imposter syndrome to own being a creative!

A long time ago, in a galaxy far, far away (Southend-on-Sea) I passed my 11 plus and went off to a girls' grammar school. I was averagely clever in this selective environment and really loved science. I also loved art. But I had to choose. Art or science? Not both. I chose science, passed a few exams and went off to King's College London to study Human Biology.

I cannot really explain how much I loved my degree. It was brilliant!

When it was time to leave, I spent a lot of time in the careers room. I was magnetically attracted to the big advertising agency grad schemes. But they were clear; in 1990, they only recruited account handlers from Oxbridge. Creatives came from Watford, and women could enter as a secretary. Yes, really.

Then, I discovered healthcare advertising as a career. I was so excited to get my first job in the creative department as a copywriter. I hadn't heard of Imposter Syndrome then, but I had it. Big time! I was daunted and fascinated by the language of art. I didn't feel like these bohemian 'creatives' who looked different to me and thought differently to me. I listened. I learned. I asked A LOT of questions. I hung out with the creatives at lunch and after work. I started going to art galleries and reading Campaign & Creative Review. I joined in with pitches and ideation.

One day my idea won a pitch. OMG! It was for a dual ingredient nasal decongestant. My idea was a clown's face with half a red nose and the headline; 'When antihistamines are only half the answer'.

I WAS a creative! I was no longer an imposter. I did it, and you can too.

Creativity is everywhere

If science is creative, and everyone is creative, then every project has some creativity within it. It's a good job you have embraced your creative self-identity because every communications project you will ever undertake has a creative dimension. The graphic below provides some examples at each end of a spectrum of medical or health communications.

Even if you are writing clinical papers or running an advisory board, there is creativity in the way you construct your arguments or agenda. There is creativity in the way you present data, or attract delegates to your scientific meeting.

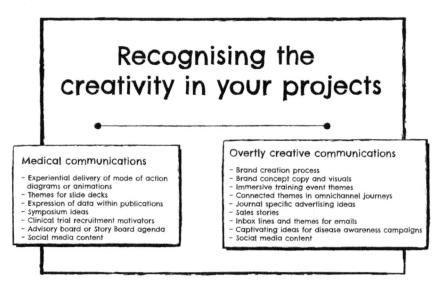

If you are dedicated to reducing cognitive load and brainpower, so your audiences say, 'I get it', creativity is your best friend. Noticing the opportunities for creativity is a great start.

How can you get your creative groove on?

Congratulations! You have noticed the creative opportunity within a project and decided to try to explore some creative options. How do you start?

- Get in the mood. Set your neurobiology up for success. Your amazing brain cannot be creative when it is stressed and flooded with adrenaline and cortisol. Harness the power of the alpha state.
- Put away your number one distraction - your phone. Tell your team you are off email for a few hours. Get away from your computer. You need to concentrate. This is important.
- Briefly look at what else is happening in the space you are thinking about – what inspires, connects with you, or moves you?
- Briefly look outside your space to other industries or therapies – who's doing something cool? Don't allow this 'research' to distract you or be an excuse for procrastination.
- Harness the power of your conscious mind. Know how you work best when engaged in active thinking. Do you write? Do you scribble or doodle? Do you record voice notes? Do you flip chart or use post-it notes?
- Harness the power of your subconscious mind. Your subconscious is vast compared with your conscious mind. I often find that if I park a problem in my head, my brain figures out what to do, without my needing to apply conscious effort. I have used this in client work and pitches by reading a new brief on a Friday. I do no active thinking that day, or over the weekend. Then, I get up early on Monday morning and actively try to solve the problem. I often find I already have lots of ideas bubbling to the surface without trying too hard. What joy!
- Know when and where you work best. I'm always intrigued by where people have their best ideas. Cycling, in the shower, in bed, drying

their hair, or driving. Where is it for you? Nobody has ever told me they have their best ideas sitting in front of a computer! We all have daily energy peaks and troughs. Notice when you're at your creative peak and try to organise your creative thinking into that time. Mornings are best for me; nowadays, my brain's too depleted for creative problem solving after 6pm.

- Work with others. Talk about the problem to be solved. Don't be too focused at the beginning. Start with as many ideas as you can (divergent thinking). Allow yourself to be a little distracted. Don't try too hard.

- Once you have lots of ideas, evaluate them against the brief, or what you are trying to achieve. Can any be made better? What can you discard? Focus on perfecting your best ideas (convergent thinking). Sometimes the first ideas are the best ones. Sometimes they are weak, but you need to get them out there, so you can go beyond them.

- Give yourself time. For most people, creative thinking does not happen so well under intense time pressures, especially at the beginning. Once you have spent many years in the role, you will get quicker. It took me at least 10 years to get to a place where I could *reliably and consistently* come up with workable ideas in a *very* short space of time.

- If you are a manager, give your team lots of opportunities to practise so they get better and better! Recognise that your organisation may never reap the fullest rewards of this. As with all training, the employee may leave long before they reach their full potential. If you believe in karma, you'll reap the rewards of someone else's training at some point. The more you give, the more you get.

- Get comfortable with failure. When we are searching for ideas, we will discard many along the way. It's perfectly OK and quite normal for some of your ideas to fall by the wayside. The point is that you are learning and contributing. Maybe a winning solution sprang from something you produced as part of the process.

Work with your neurobiology, not against it. Give your brain, and everyone else's, the best chance of creative success.

The alpha state, Lego and a brick experiment

Neuroscientists have discovered that higher alpha brain wave activity correlates with people's ability to come up with less obvious or well known ideas.[10]

Try this experiment. Get together with at least two other people and two decent sized piles of Lego. Set a timer for five minutes and set each team off on the following:

Person or group 1
Makes something from their Lego

Person or group 2
Sorts the Lego into piles by colour

Person or group 3
Sits doing nothing, but not watching the other teams

At the end of five minutes, each person or group must come up with as many uses for a house brick as they can think of.

You should find that the group that sorts the bricks by colour comes up with way more creative uses for a house brick than the other teams.

Mundane or undemanding tasks can help us enter an almost meditative state. Have you noticed you tend to think of lots of things when you are pairing socks, peeling veg, ironing or gardening?

Creating brands

Some of you will be involved in creating a brand from scratch. That process is another book, but here are some tips for creating brand concepts.

Ensure your words and pictures are complimentary. They should work together for a complete communication. If the headline simply describes the visual, you have wasted an opportunity.

Create an emotional connection. Your campaign should make the audience 'feel' something. When you have a great idea, you will feel the emotion too. I have sometimes shed a little tear when I have written a great ad. Sometimes I have laughed. I have even made myself angry. Healthcare professionals will always say they prefer rational campaigns over emotional ones. Many marketeers believe them. Let me remind you that healthcare professionals are humans on the inside. They respond to emotional brand campaigns as humans, not machines. The evidence on this speaks for itself. Emotional campaigns outperform rational ones over the long term.

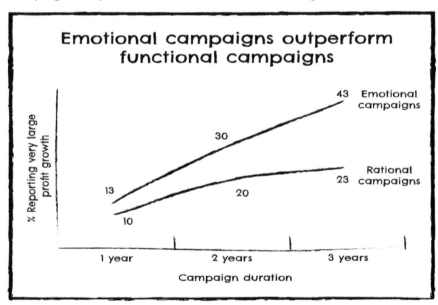

Adapted from: The Long and the Short of It, Binet & Field, IPA, 2013.

Market research can evaluate the emotional impact of a campaign. Brands like John Lewis have been doing it for years. If you want to create an emotional connection, but are not sure what emotion is appropriate to elicit, check out Plutchik's wheel of emotion.

Robert Plutchik was a psychologist whose work is often used today to help people understand their emotions. It's all over the internet, you can use it for inspiration. At Wordbird, we include emotional objectives in our brief template to guide our communication goals.

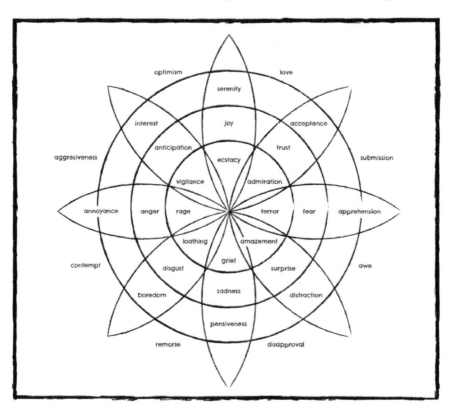

I hope you feel inspired to reconnect with your inner creative. Trust it is in there. Know you are already using it in many areas of your life. Be gentle with your brain and give it the best chance of success ☺

The power of a label
If you are a manager or a leader consider how you 'label' your writers.

- Are they part of the creative department?
- Do they have plenty of contact with The Creative Director and access to the creative process?
- Do you encourage them to work through ideas with art directors or designers?
- What creative expectations do you set?
- Do you involve them in discussions about creative aspects of a job
- What's your creative training?

If you are ever frustrated that your writers are not as creative as you would like, ask yourself whether you have set them up for success. There is a lot you can do to set up a creative environment that offers your writers the best chance of unleashing their creativity. Are you doing it?

'I get it' moments on being a creative and the power of ideas

- Science is creative. You are creative. You have every right to call yourself a creative. Move on!
- Almost every project has an opportunity for creativity. Look out for the opportunities because they have the power to reduce the cognitive load/brain power required by your audience and increase the chance that they will 'get it'.
- Work with your brain to maximise your chances of creative success.
- Brand campaigns that evoke an emotional response perform better in the long term than rational ones – healthcare professionals may disagree! Don't forget they are human on the inside!

CHAPTER 8

Mastery Zone 6: explaining and presenting your work
- how you show up

Once you have some easy-to-understand creative ideas that brilliantly solve your brief, your work is done, right? Wrong. Your next challenge is to bring everyone else along with you, inside your agency first and with clients next. The most successful creatives are either naturally gifted in this; or they have worked hard to make it look effortless; or they work with others who are brilliant communicators. So which one are you now? And what are you going to be in the future?

Let's consider a scenario from two perspectives.

An account manager, let's call him Bertrand, has briefed you, the writer, on a patient website home page. He has explained what the client wants to achieve, what the challenges are, and has provided you with a comprehensive written brief. You agree to meet again in three days to share your ideas.

For the next three days, you work up two or three ideas and content plans. You have a chat with a designer and they layer in some visual ideas to make the ideas even better. You're working on a few other jobs, but this is the uppermost one in your mind. You are really chuffed with your engagement ideas and are excited to share them with Bertrand and your creative director, Marjorie.

While you are working on the brief, Bertrand has been working on final delivery for a large congress. The deadlines are tight. The booth is stuck in Italian Customs.

The signatories have requested last minute changes to the speaker slides and one of the expert panel is sick. Life has been pretty brutal for Bertrand, but you have no idea about all this.

The meeting starts, and you excitedly show your ideas. But oh dear. Bertrand and Marjorie do not leap to their feet, applauding wildly. They look confused. They start asking you lots of questions about the brief. You feel like you are going backwards. When they finally understand your ideas, it feels a bit flat. The joy is no longer there.

The reason, my friend, is simple. You have made too many assumptions and not brought your team along with you. You have forgotten that Bertrand and Marjorie are human beings!

- You assumed Bertrand remembered the details of the brief he shared with you three days ago
- You assumed Marjorie had prepared for the meeting by reading the brief
- When you were showing your ideas, they were trying to remember or understand the objective. They couldn't do this and listen to you. It was really hard work for them.
- You assumed that others could see inside your mind and that all the considerations and thinking would be obvious.

The truth is that after Bertrand and Marjorie had spent a lot of brainpower remembering or understanding the brief, you didn't explain your proposal. All that thought, the ideas you dismissed, the research and deep thinking, was not evident. And because they could not see your effort, they wrongly assumed you had not put in much work.

I know this is very unfair. But knowledge is power, and you need to know how to bring people along!

Here's how I would structure the sharing of ideas internally or with clients to make it easy for them, so you show your work in the best possible light.

1. Re-orientation

Human beings have busy brains and even busier lives. The first part of presenting any work is reorientation. This must be short. Your audience wants to get to the solutions and will have a limited 'concentration window' for re-orientation. You need to quickly remind them of:

- The project and objective
- What behaviour change you are trying to elicit
- The strategy to achieve this
- How you want the target audience to feel
- Anything that has a significant influence on the project e.g. limited time or budget, compliance restrictions, new insights or specific requests or requirements

Allow any clarification discussions to happen before you show *anything*.

If you don't have the luxury of a meeting to share your ideas, I would always put re-orientation information in my PowerPoint deck, or in my covering email. Even better, do a video of your screen with an audio commentary (walkthrough video). Once everyone is clear on the brief, move to ideas.

2. Explain your ideas or proposal

In the example above, the ideas were shown rather than explained. But explanation is what is needed, and it's probably more than you think.

- Briefly explain how you went about this work. What were your inspirations? What are you bringing from outside the brief? What was your thought process? What did you dismiss and why? Show how deeply you have thought about the challenge. If it was hard, say so. If it was fun, or inspiring, say that too. If there was a part of the brief that you really struggled to execute, share your concerns and suggestions for improvements.

- Careful presentation will show what you have personally invested and how much effort you have put in. When people see how much you care, they are more likely to be on your side from the outset. I might say:

"I have really enjoyed working on this brief and it made me think of a report I was reading in The British Medical Journal…"

"This is a tricky brief, but a starting point could lay in some inspiration from a reel I saw on Instagram"

"I have read all the papers you supplied and done a quick Pubmed search myself. The common thread is [_____] so I have woven that in as a theme"

"The research was really helpful. On page 64 there was a quote that made me think we could approach the content like this…"

"We know that doctors want to know [_____] so the content plan directly satisfies this requirement"

- Then talk through the proposals. Start with the bigger picture and summarise each option in a few words, or couple of sentences. Then go to the next level. Share your plan, ideas or a theme in headlines. Allow time for discussion and questions. Then move to the detail. Show that you have considered everything. Listen carefully with an open heart. You are not perfect; there will be gaps at this early stage, so jot them down for your refinement stage. Often your team will want some reflection or processing time. In this case, ask for first impressions and set up a follow up session.

- Sometimes, especially at the early stages, you will be way off beam with your first thoughts. That's OK. It's all part of the learning process. It's important to get used to plenty of feedback, but there is no doubt this can be very hard, especially if you are an extreme perfectionist. I love this quote, currently attributed to Cheryl Cole online, but frequently cited by my late father-in-law decades before Cheryl claimed it!

"I have learned so much from my mistakes I am thinking of making some more."

Do good ideas and good thinking speak for themselves?

Throughout your career, people will tell you that good ideas don't need explaining. They should speak for themselves.

I agree that in the final execution, seen by the final audience, this is true.

However, on the way to that point, there will be many people seeing early stages; agency teams, marketing clients, medical clients, sometimes other agencies, and everyone involved in the execution.

They are not seeing the final version. They are imagining their version of the vision. If you don't share the thinking and the vision, everyone will have a different vision. This is the unwitting path to disappointment and disaster.

> ## The perils of perfectionism
>
> We all want to do a good job and avoid mistakes. A dose of healthy perfectionism can drive us to overcome adversity and achieve success.
>
> But take care! Extreme perfectionism creates a focus on avoiding failure and harsh judgement. Extreme perfectionism is common in healthcare communications because of the high level of attention to detail required.
>
> "Perfectionists set unrealistically high expectations for themselves and others. They are quick to find fault and overly critical of mistakes. They tend to procrastinate out of their fear of failure. They shrug off compliments and forget to celebrate their successes. Instead, they look to specific people in their life for approval and validation."[11]
>
> If you are a person with high attention to detail, extreme perfectionism is always a danger. Recognising and managing this tendency is important as it will hold you back.

In the early days of your career, more senior members of your team will often present your work to clients. You might not even go to the meeting. Even more reason to ensure that they understand how you approached the challenge and all the effort you have put into it.

Summarise the next steps

After you have shared your ideas, there will probably be some discussion. Your ideas might spark new ideas bouncing all over the place. It might be quite scattergun. You might find it hard to follow. Listen and take notes.

When the discussion is coming to an end, say you'd like to summarise the next steps.

This could be:

- What is working well
- What needs more refinement
- What is not working so well and won't be progressed
- If any new approaches are needed
- Whether there's some new thinking to weave in
- If there's something you had not thought about and now need to incorporate

In my experience, few people remember the specifics agreed in these meetings without written notes. Your notes will often be a synthesis of what you heard, plus usually some explicit instructions. These notes take effort, but they are solid gold to start the next internal meeting's re-orientation.

My 'insider info' is that agency people often hate writing up these 'next steps', so if you take this on, everyone will love you. And that is quite important.

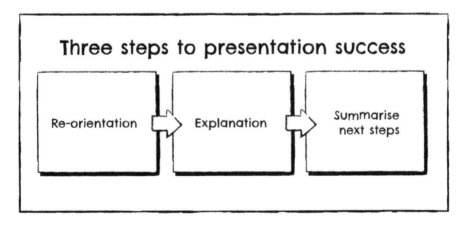

Presentation of content is a skill. Rocking up to an internal meeting without planning increases the risk that your work will be rejected, or you might not be taken seriously. Once you have proved yourself within your agency, seek out opportunities to present to clients using the same excellent processes you have developed internally.

> ### Be brief, be bright, be gone
>
> At times you will be presenting to senior people with very little time. They often want you to 'be brief, be bright and be gone!' It's not unusual to get just 45 minutes to present a whole pitch. The first time this happened to me I was shocked. And insulted. How could we condense weeks of great thinking into 45 minutes? But it can be done. Of course, it takes longer and lots more effort to make something shorter, but it's a great way to showcase your talents.
>
> There are lots of these people in our industry. Sometimes I'm one of them!
>
> Here are three top tips:
> 1. Prepare far more carefully so you can only focus on what matters most
> 2. Make the set up succinct, focussing on the client, not you
> 3. Get to solutions fast and minimise chit chat
> 4. Bring energy, enthusiasm and pace!

How you show up matters

Presenting your work with credibility, conviction, and confidence is just one aspect of building trust with your team and your clients.

My prediction is that your career progression will be strongly correlated with the level of trust others have in you. I have no mathematical proof of this. It's just my theory. The good news is that you can control some of the 'trust variables'. And it comes down to how you show up. Crikey! What on earth does that mean?

'Showing up' in this context is a relatively new term for me. It means how you 'reveal yourself'. In a work context, this refers to the work, the task, you do and the way you go about it, your human skills, or the way you relate to others. When we start our work lives, we tend to be very task orientated. Here are some ways that trust is built in relation to tasks.

- High quality work (clear, compliant, creative etc)
- Sticking to timeline and budget
- Being pragmatic, organised and methodical

Task-orientated trust is built on important functional qualities. As we progress, we learn that it's not all about the task.

Trust is also built through human skills. We used to call these 'soft skills'. I am a serious fan of Simon Sinek. Check out his genius books and 'A bit of Optimism' podcast. Simon Sinek has coined the better phrase, 'human skills', to describe how we relate to each other. Good 'human skills' build deep trust. And deep trust is critical for high performing teams.

Here are some examples of human skills in an agency:

- Proactively providing your team with updates on how you are getting on so they don't worry about progress and keep bothering you for updates
- Giving and receiving compliments about nice work or helpful actions
- Feeling safe to make an active contribution in meetings

- Having the courage to ask for help when you are stuck, or don't know what to do
- Knowing what you need and how to ask for it positively
- Nicely drawing people's attention to a problem or mistake, without drama or blame
- Tuning into what others need from you
- Providing feedback to others in a way that inspires
- Bringing positive energy and being conscious of your energy levels – enjoying work and bringing the fun
- Having good habits to replenish your energy levels and noticing the dangers of energy depletion
- Working on self-awareness and keeping out of the drama triangle

Drama triangle

This concept from psychology is one of the most helpful things I have ever learned to help me understand myself and others.

This model was proposed by Stephen Karpman to explain the behaviour of people in conflict. You can easily look it up online.

Conflict can be overt or more 'polite'. It might be that you don't gel with a colleague, a boss, or you feel overwhelmed. In the drama triangle, people become the 'victim', 'martyr' or 'persecutor'.

At some point in your career, things will not go so well. Maybe a client relationship is breaking down, or maybe one of your team is having a difficult time. Whatever the cause, recognising the behaviours in the drama triangle will help you develop strategies to avoid being drawn in.

Here's an example. Imagine a client who had not chosen to work with your agency. Let's call him Percy. Percy didn't have the courage to say he'd prefer to work with another agency. So he quietly seethed and played the martyr. Because he wanted you to fail, he did not set you up for success. Everything you did was wrong, as far as Percy was concerned. He became a persecutor. Even worse, when you presented costs, he switched to victim mode and pleaded for a reduction.

Recognising that Percy is not his best self and is stuck in the drama triangle can help you avoid being drawn into the opposite role e.g. victim to his persecutor.

Personally, I dislike conflict, so being able to change my own energy around others is a useful tool for me. This is a good example of how managing yourself can help you progress.

Your whole self, your best self and your worst self

None of us can separate work and life. Work is a big part of life, but do our work colleagues see part of who we are, or our 'whole self'.

I have worked with people who reveal very little of their home lives at work and people who share everything. Really, everything!

It's a personal decision. All I would say is that keeping a big part of your life 'secret' from your colleagues takes a lot of energy. I have worked with people who have never spoken about really 'big stuff'; relationship breakdowns, being gay, absence of childcare when they were trying to work, or having another job 'on the side'. When my kids were small a colleague told me to leave 'mum-me' at the office door. So (mostly) I did.

But here's the thing. Everyone feels when something is 'off'. People know when someone is not their best self and they descend into 'The Drama Triangle'.

When I am stressed, or trying too hard to be a good leader, or feel I'm being judged unfairly, I have too. We all do. Fortunately the science of psychology helps us understand ourselves and manage ourselves.

Human skills are very sophisticated skills! But guess what, they are also linked with happiness!

Human skills don't always come naturally and require practise and intention. Lots of us develop these skills through coaching, having some training, or joining an organisation specialising in personal growth.

'I get it' moments on explaining and presenting your work and how you show up

- Take great care in bringing everyone along and sharing your work
- Re-orientate, explain (don't show), summarise next steps
- Know when to be bright, be brief, and be gone!
- Prepare harder when time is short
- Build trust through mastery of the task and mastery of your human skills

CHAPTER 9

Mastery Zone 7: developing yourself and managing yourself

I hope the title of this chapter has thrown you a bit. I'm sure you're super-interested in developing yourself so you can grow and progress. Many people progress without ever learning how to manage themselves. You'll know them. They are the ones who can be a nightmare to work with. Egotistical, demeaning, ruthless, unhelpful, confusing. Then there are those who get 'stuck' at a certain level, doing lots of training, but not really progressing. In my experience, the writers who do the very best are great at understanding themselves *and* managing themselves. Sounds a bit woo woo?

Let your curiosity lead you on...

Traditional career development

Let's start with the easy bit. If you are a relatively new writer, you should expect training. In my opinion, this should be a mix of 'lessons' and 'on the job training'.

In my agency, a trainee writer in their first year will record between 200-300 hours of CPD. You need to know about all the following:

- The therapeutic area(s) and accounts you will be working in
- Formal Code of Practice Training
- Your agency processes, confidentiality and data protection
- Stages of a job
- Copy and stylesheet
- Claims and referencing
- Checking

In my agency, a writer's six month induction also covers many of the things in this book:

- Plain English and readability
- Medicines' landscape – how drugs are developed and regulated
- What to do when you make a mistake
- What to do when you don't know what to do
- What a brand is
- Write from wrong
- Tone of voice
- How to become your own best editor
- Visual communication and design principles
- Storytelling and strategic writing
- Uploading to Veeva, Pepperflow, or other approval systems
- Human skills
- IPA Foundation Certificate

In a busy agency, it can be hard to fit all this in. Flexibility and determination are required from the trainer *and the trainee*. The trainee, YOU, must take responsibility for driving their own development and reminding if things have slipped. I LOVE it when people remind me I have forgotten something, and your boss will too!

This 'basic training' should be built upon over the coming years, so you get to the point where you can do whole jobs independently and present them yourself with credibility and conviction.

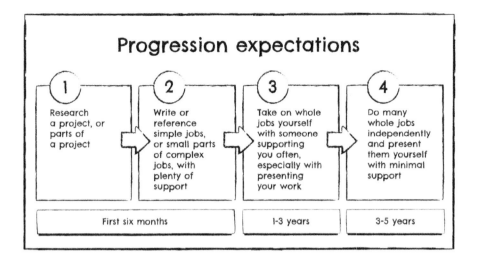

The IPA (Institute of Practitioners in Advertising) the professional body for advertisers and communication agencies, requires that its member agency staff complete at least 24 hours of Continuing Professional Development (CPD) every year. I believe you should expect to complete WAY more than this, whatever stage of your career you are in. Most years, I spend over 200 hours developing myself or others. Training is any time you are learning something you did not know before, or working on personal growth:

- Researching a new therapeutic category
- 1:1s with your manager or coach
- Reading development books, watching Ted Talks, attending webinars, Meet-ups or listening to podcasts
- Attending conferences
- Taking part in formal training or gaining a professional qualification

There was a time when there was almost no formal training for writers. An agency's training budget was almost exclusively focused on client service. Who knows why that was?

Today copywriters can consider:

- Presentation skills
- D&AD (Design and Art Direction) courses
- Creative evaluation
- Data visualisation
- Professional marketing/Digital marketing qualifications
- Behavioural economics and communication
- How to sell or persuade
- Association of British Science Writer events
- Plain English Campaign courses
- Plus so much more besides

Once you start noticing the opportunities, you won't be able to stop!

The most important thing is to link your training to your development plan. At Wordbird we call reviews, Previews. That's because they are not just retrospective, but prospective too. The prospective part is your goals. Goals, or objectives, need to be mutually beneficial. Let me say that again. *Mutually beneficial.* You need to ensure your boss can see a benefit to their business when you achieve your goals. Your boss will be super-impressed if you can tie your goal to your agency strategy or annual goals.

Here are two examples of goals; some training to support and the employer benefit:

Goal for a writer in the first three years: In the next six months, I will improve my data visualisation skills so that I can better represent client data in my work. This will be measured by my manager noticing improvement and positive client feedback.

Training: I will attend an online data visualisation webinar, write up 5 things I learned, share these with my colleagues and practise whenever I am writing on client jobs.

The cost is £500. The potential return on investment for the agency: more ability to surprise and delight clients by bringing their data to life in a way that they can process and remember it.

Goal for a more experienced writer beyond 3-5 years: In the next year I will increase my understanding of digital marketing outside healthcare so I can maximise the opportunities for omnichannel solutions within our client's omnichannel platforms.

Training: I will gain a qualification in Professional Digital Marketing and share key learnings and implications with my colleagues, so these can be integrated into at least three proposals.

The cost is £2000. I propose that we share the cost, and I am requesting 14 hours of paid study leave. The potential return on investment for the agency is being able to enhance our client recommendations to maximise the most up-to-date opportunities.

Managing yourself and personal growth

In the section on how you 'show up', I explained that trust is based on competency in functional skills (doing your job) and human skills (how you manage yourself and relate to others).

Managing yourself means you can:

- Manage your energy and work fruitfully and without procrastination
- Manage your time
- Recognise what help you need and ask for it
- Handle setbacks, disappointment, difficult feedback and difficult people
- Know your boundaries and when to break them
- Know how to manage overwhelm
- Avoid burnout
- And most importantly, enjoy your successes!

The bad news is that I cannot teach you these skills in this book. I can draw your attention to the fact that, at some point, you will need to know how to do all of these things, and more, no matter where your career takes you. That's why they are called human skills!

> ## Questions for curious clients
>
> Better trained staff do a better job for their clients. So it always surprises me that so few clients, considering working with us, ever ask about training. Maybe they assume all agencies have high quality training.
>
> If you are a curious client, here are some good questions to ask your agency:
>
> - Does everyone working on your account have regular Code training?
> - Does anyone working on your account have a marketing qualification?
> - What training do your writers receive, in addition to 'on the job' training?
>
> I rather suspect that you may be met with some bluster, smoke and mirrors. I imagine some agency people will be very unhappy with me encouraging you to ask these questions.

Burnout

Sometimes we all have unrealistic ideas about what is possible within the time available.

Sometimes there is an important deadline that demands extraordinary working and long hours to get the job done on time. My favourite example of this was doing a launch campaign in 14 working days. Everything that would normally take a week was done in a day. It was intense, fun and a brilliant client agency-partnership. I bloody loved it! It is very normal in agency life to need to put your own life on hold every now and again for the benefit of patients. I reframe it as a privilege.

But this way of working is unsustainable as a usual, everyday practice. It is extraordinary effort for occasional circumstances. Humans cannot sustain this pace for everyday working.

People who deplete their energy and do not replenish it burn out. Check out the 12 stages of burnout online. Sadly, it is VERY common in our industry, especially among women.

I have burnt out several times. Most recently, in the pandemic, I was working a 70-hour week, giving every KJ of my energy to my team, my clients, steering my business through rough seas and looking after my family and son, who was seriously ill. I was doing very little to replenish my energy levels and, at 52, my hormones were in freefall. I found 10 hours a day at a screen exhausting even though some days I only walked 200 steps. I was overweight, drinking half a bottle of wine a day. I was my worst self – a superwoman caught in the drama triangle as a martyr. But I did not have this self-awareness at the time.

> The good news is that this misery reignited my passion for personal growth. I joined a lifestyle programme called Second Nature, lost 10kg and began to prioritise my own self care. I upped my HRT, and once the gyms opened, danced my way back to fitness. No more wine and a whine! Now I celebrate every single tiny success. I joined a women's leadership organisation called One of Many, where I learned some amazing new techniques to manage my energy, my relationships and my money.
>
> Then I Co-Founded Women in Pharma (with the very fabulous Miriam Kenrick) an organisation to inspire and empower the amazing women working in pharma to shake the future of women's health.

At some point, once the functional stuff is under control, you will feel ready to work on your human skills. You might start this by listening to some podcasts, or reading some books. If you're not sure where to start, try podcasts by Rangan Chattergee or Adam Grant. I have heard that the Loose Women in Pharma podcast is pretty good too.

You might decide to invest in yourself by getting a coach. Better still, you might ask your employer to pay for your coach. Whatever you decide, don't think you have human skills nailed. They are never nailed. We are never fully trained or 'finished'. But we can continue to grow. Growth can be exciting *and* very uncomfortable. That's because to grow, you must leave your comfort zone and enter the 'uncomfortable' zone. After a while, the uncomfortable zone becomes your new comfort zone. Like a fluffy pillow and a warm duvet. Delicious! Enjoy it for a while. You'll 'feel' when you need to seek a new 'uncomfortable' zone again.

If there is anything I regret, it is the mid-15 years of my career when personal growth and managing myself were not a priority for me. Maybe I held myself back like so many women do, getting in my own way. I did great work in that time and grew creatively and academically, but on reflection, it was not enough. I share this mistake freely, so you won't make the same one.

> ## How women hold themselves back
>
> It is possible for men and women to get in their own way when it comes to career development. But the things that hold men and women back are different.
>
> In the book 'How Women Rise' by Sally Helgesen and Marshall Goldsmith, the authors identify 12 habits holding women back from their next promotion, pay rise or job. It's a great read.
>
> One of the key themes is that women struggle to claim their own accomplishments. Female employees tend to be conscientious, producing work of a very high standard. Their weakness lies in their discomfort with drawing attention to their successes. It is very typical for women to share credit with a team, rather than acknowledge their hard work in front of senior colleagues. Other social conditioning ideas, like people pleasing, perfectionism, and the need for excessive expertise, are traits that specifically limit women.

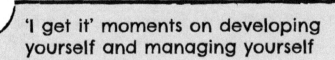

'I get it' moments on developing yourself and managing yourself

- Personal development means learning how to do the job and how to manage yourself
- Trust is based on competency in functional skills (doing your job) and human skills (how you manage yourself and relate to others)
- Hold your boss, or trainer, to account on training plans and if you are not doing at least 24 hours of CPD each year, ask yourself why - and what the consequences are
- Training is anything where you learn something new
- The drama triangle is a good model to understand why some people behave 'badly', including yourself
- Seek the 'uncomfortable zone', for that is where the magic happens

CHAPTER 10

What next?

I hope you agree that we should make it marvellously easy for all health audiences to say, 'I get it'. And that you're inspired to make your difference in the world, armed with the knowledge to do all the right things, crusading against jargon and minimising the cognitive load or brain power you demand of your readers. Thank you for reading my book. It's been a pleasure to write. I wanted to make it marvellously easy for you to say 'I get it' too, so just to be clear, here's what I would say to my 21 year old self…

> Know your evidence. Know your code,
> Minimise the cognitive load.
>
> Keep it short. Never long.
> Always champion 'Write from Wrong'!
>
> Develop your skills, develop yourself,
> Be sure to prioritise *your own* health,
>
> Have a mentor, then get a coach,
> Try hard to be beyond reproach.
>
> Manage your energy and your time,
> Take care to avoid a wine and a whine!
>
> Face every challenge knowing your strengths,
> Sometimes go to extraordinary lengths.
>
> Work hard. Have fun,
> Congratulate yourself when a job's well done.

Explain things nicely – bring others along,
Win awards! You can get those gongs!

Show up and lead with intention,
Remember, humour always diffuses tension.

Be nervous of jargon and acro-nyms
Heck! They're not even rhyming things!

Own your mistakes.
Eat plenty of cakes!

See clients as friends. And never foe.
Know when jobs should stop and when to go!

Be curious! Always know your 'why',
Have sensible boundaries - and when not to apply.

Embrace AI. But don't trust it, yet.
When things go wrong, try not to fret.

Seek the wisdom of the crowd, but know your own mind too.
Ask for help when you don't know what to do.

When patients get the best from a medicine or device
Everything's worth it – the hard work! The strife!

You've given your best, you didn't quit,
Now it's marvellously easy to say, 'I get it!'

References

1. National Library of Medicine. Physiology, Explicit Memory. Available at: **https://www.ncbi.nlm.nih.gov/books/NBK554551/**. Accessed January 2024.
2. Sweller J. Cognitive Science 1988; 12(2): 257-85.
3. Leppink J *et al*. Behav Res 2013 45: 1058–72.
4. National Institute for Health and Care Research. Health information: are you getting your message across? Available at: **https://evidence.nihr.ac.uk/collection/health-information-are-you-getting-your-message-across/**. Accessed January 2024.
5. The Pharmaceutical Journal. Drug development: the journey of a medicine from lab to shelf. Available at: **https://pharmaceutical-journal.com/article/feature/drug-development-the-journey-of-a-medicine-from-lab-to-shelf**. Accessed January 2024.
6. Gaesser B. Front Psychol 2013; 3: doi: 10.3389/fpsyg.2012.00576
7. San José State University Writing Centre. Sentence Variety and Rhythm. Available at: **https://www.sjsu.edu/writingcenter/docs/handouts/Sentence%20Variety%20and%20Rhythm.pdf**. Accessed January 2024.
8. Baynard Institute. Readability: The Optimal Line Length. Available at: **https://baymard.com/blog/line-length-readability**. Accessed January 2024.
9. Clear J. Atomic Habits 2008. ISBN: 9780735211292. Available at: **https://businesswales.gov.wales/sites/maingel2/files/documents/Atomic%20Habits%20-%20James%20Clear%202018_0.pdf**. Accessed January 2024.
10. Di Bernardi Luft C *et al*. PNAS 2018; 115(52): E12144-E12152.
11. Psychology Today. Perfectionism. Available at: **https://www.psychologytoday.com/gb/basics/perfectionism**. Accessed January 2024.

Beyond 'Bikini Medicine'

Published in The Medicine Maker 2024

Hello again! Welcome to another Women in Pharma missive to challenge your thinking!

Boom! Let's get right in with 'Bikini Medicine'. What on earth is that? Well, it's the mistaken belief that women's health only differs from men's in the parts of the body that a bikini would cover. Of course, reproductive and breast health is very important, but what about the rest of a woman's body?

When you are thinking about your work in medicines, devices, medtech, patient programmes or clinical trials, how often do you think about men and women's 'whole body' physiology differently?

No, until recently, us neither. Like most of you, we were *unconsciously* working within the deep-seated, societal belief, that women are essentially men with different reproductive organs. Of course, this is nonsense and makes no sense when you take a *conscious*, scientific perspective! We all know that every cell in a woman's body is different to a man's because women have two XX chromosomes. But strangely, that doesn't provoke us to ask gender-based questions about medical solutions.

The evidence tells us that women and men experience many diseases differently and at different rates. According to leading neuroscientist Dr Lisa Mosconi, in her 2020 book 'The XX brain'

- "Women are twice as likely to have anxiety and depression as men.

- Women are over three times more likely than men to be diagnosed with an autoimmune disorder, including those that attack the brain, like multiple sclerosis.
- Women are up to four times more likely to suffer from migraines and headaches than men
- Women are more prone than men to develop meningiomas, the most common brain tumours.
- Strokes kill more women than men."

As if this is not bad enough, Dr Mosconi goes on to explain that, looking further through the neuroscience lens, Alzheimer's is the biggest threat to women's health; *two out of every three Alzheimer's patients are women*. Women in their 60s are about *twice as likely to develop Alzheimer's as they are to develop breast cancer*. Yet Alzheimer's is not labelled as a women's health issue.

Pioneering women are calling to us all to recognise that diseases that affect both men and women may present differently.

Today, scientists are required to recruit both men and women for research. This wasn't always the case. For decades after the thalidomide scandal, research was overwhelmingly conducted on male cells, male mice and male patients. This supplied medicine with data that discounted 51% of the population. 'Normal' meant 'male'.

According to Dr Mosconi, today important indicators of gender differentials are often statistically removed from studies. Dr Mosconi says:

"In order to look at men and women independently, studies would need twice the number of patients, twice the time and twice the money. Many scientists have no other option than to keep removing gender from the equation, suppressing its undeniable impact on study outcomes." Hmmm. This feels very uncomfortable.

But there is an upside. We have chatted with Women in Pharma who design clinical studies. They have told us it is well within the capabilities of our amazing industry to be more ambitious in clinical study design and analysis.

Women in Pharma is encouraging you to look beyond 'Bikini Medicine'. As inspiration, let's look at oestrogen in a different way. The neuroscience lens shows oestrogen as the 'master regulator' of the brain, with many functions BEYOND reproduction: energy regulation, neuro-protection, mood, endorphins and cardiovascular management. The effect of oestrogen in women, and testosterone in men, means our brains have different levels of neurotransmitters, different cellular make ups and different connectivity in some regions. If the 'master regulator' of the body is different, surely other things are different too?

And we have some evidence about drugs. Most famously, men and women taking the same doses of the sleeping pill zolpidem, have dramatically different reactions. Women are more likely to sleepwalk, sleep eat and even sleep drive. Women reach maximum blood levels of this drug at much lower doses than men.

When this came to light, the FDA halved the recommended dose for women, but for the previous 20 years, women had been compromised by overmedication.

Whatever your gender, Women in Pharma is challenging YOU to ask:

- Does the disease I work in affect men and women differently?
- How will we bring this knowledge into our study designs and outcomes?
- Are there any barriers to recruiting enough men and women to trials to power analysis of sex differences in drug performance?

- Could gender-based *post-hoc* analyses of large trials tell us more about the performance of existing drugs?
- Are we asking how the menstrual cycle, hormonal contraception, or the menopause affect the performance of our drug?

In an era of personalised medicine, your findings might better serve women AND men. Imagine the possibilities. What if:

- Underperformance in women drags down results in men for a drug that works brilliantly for them
- You found your drug had safety signals for women, but not for men
- Your medicine had low efficacy in men and so it was denied to women for whom it transformed lives

Women in Pharma is calling to men and women in pharma, biotech, medtech and beyond to go beyond the bikini and ask themselves, 'What do those XX chromosomes in every cell in a woman's body really mean for medicine?'

The XX Brain by Dr Lisa Mosconi. The Groundbreaking Science Empowering Women to Prevent Dementia.

Join the Women in Pharma database so we can email you
https://forms.gle/tEott6vi1749wTdW6

Join the Women in Pharma LinkedIn group
https://www.linkedin.com/groups/12706819/

Try our Loose Women in Pharma podcast which we're told people particularly enjoy. All kinds of conversations happen here
so be warned!
https://itunes.apple.com/WebObjects/MZStore.woa/wa/viewPodcast?id=1656797527

Acknowledgements

I have learned so much from so many people. There's a bit of them all in this book.

My wonderful Wordbird team. Every single person who we have ever employed has taught me something valuable. I never stop learning from you all. Kat Gridley, I cannot thank you enough for backing me in writing this book.

Miriam Kenrick, my Women in Pharma Co-Founder - my soul sister and work wife, who shares my conviction that we can all change the world.

Louisa Pau, business coach. You have believed in me even when I didn't believe in myself. You noticed when I burnt out and set me on the road to recovery. I could not have achieved half of what I have without your wisdom.

Rina Newton, Co-Founder of Code Clarity, who expertly reviewed my compliance content.

My early mentors Lesley Bushnell, Sandy Wilson, Frank Walters, John Wilson and John Timney.

Kait Ayres who included me in some of our industry's very earliest multichannel campaigns, encouraged me to set up Wordbird and showed me what forensic attention to detail really is!

The late, great Carmel Thomson, Grand Duchess of Copy, inspiration, friend and creative muse.

My lovely sister, Dr Emma Sowerby. Fertility champion and my greatest cheerleader and support.

My late father-in-law, Brian Nicholson, who understood how tough and painful it is to run a business - and how to survive it.

My husband and business partner, Andrew Nicholson. A man of ideas. Creative in every cell of his body. The yin to my yang. Thank you for making all the crazy ideas happen and being such a brilliant dad to Josh and Ollie, especially when I was an unconventional mum!

Our amazing sons, who will always be our greatest achievement.

Wordbird services

Wordbird is a **full service creative healthcare agency** helping clients to devise and execute brilliant, insight-driven ideas.

We take **clinical data** and transform it into **strategic, emotive, creative content** with **multichannel** engagement.

You can rely on our expertise in **brand development** and **storytelling** to help you **communicate** with your audience in a way that is always clear and meaningful.

Our purpose is to make it marvellously easy for everyone to say "I get it".

Printed in Great Britain
by Amazon